Published by:

The Professional Image, Inc.

In the U.S.: South Beach and South Florida

International: St. Croix, St. Thomas, Tortola, St. Maarten, Aruba

Contact us at: foodbrat@gmail.com

Ebook isbn: 978-1-5323-4619-4

Print book ISBN: 978-1-5323-4618-7

Thanks to our Staff:

Photographers: The Professional Image, Inc.

The Professional Image, Inc.

Ordering Information:

Quantity sales: Special discounts are available on quantity purchases by corporations, associations, and others. For details, contact the publisher at the address above.

Orders by U.S. trade bookstores and wholesalers. Please contact TPI

Published and Printed in the United States of America

I want

the *Part* of *You*

that you *Refuse* to

give to *Anyone* else.

To love someone like you...
is to truly be alive.

I have stayed silent in my own corner of my
life too long;

I ask myself why I have love no longer;

It is not wine, woman and song that as a
younger man I once choose;

I ask myself to look into my soul why I am I in
this situation now;

Because when I had love, I drove it away!

Since I have found that abandoned LOVE, a
deaden heart flutters once
again;

I think of you,
my heart races, when I see your picture,
a smile widens;

When I finally see your beautiful eyes and are
so close I can hear your heart pulse;

Then I will truly be alive!

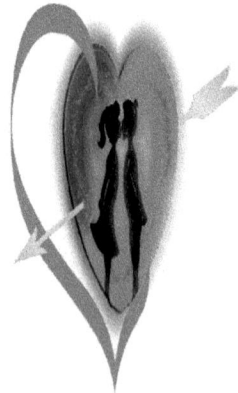

Table of Contents:

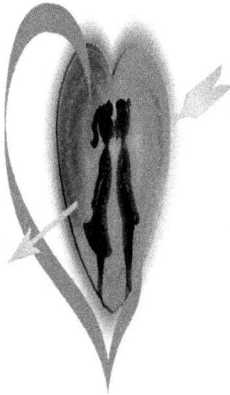

....Kiss me like the

first time that we ever

kissed and then I want

you to Kiss me more

like it is our last time that

we Ever do this again.

Prelude:

Love is Torture

You are my Addiction:

....to say you haven't been my addiction; is a needless use of Words.

I have been thinking about my _First_ love...

... you created a spark inside my soul; that is now a frenzied fire.

~ now I burn;

_B_urn with desire for you; it is only _You_!

....I have stopped thinking about women;

it is only you!

... in a world filled with beautiful _W_oman;

it is only you!

.....now I think little about other diversions

and now;

I only think about _You_;

it is only you!

... while dreaming about making love to you;

it is only you!

~ I feel love _Again_;

it is only you!

...I am not trying to be something I am not;

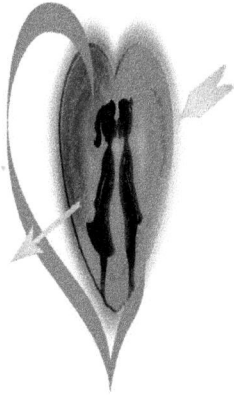

-I am just striving to live without you here;

... in hope that someday this will change.

~ Our life together has grown

.... *CApart* ...

...Although we'd have grown, we have grown
CAlone!

~ You say I am the same but,

....It has been too long since we were one;

- *CAre* we...

.... are we the same as before?

~ I see you in pictures and I fall for you all over again;

... falling - in love - with a *Beautiful* woman that
was once my wife.

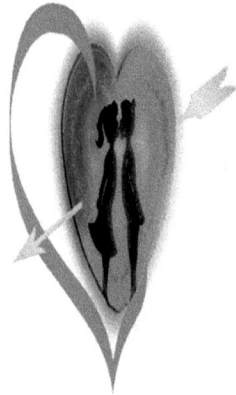

~ It is like a *Starting* over....

...thinking about how we were earlier in our lives;

- about how we made love *Every* day,

.... just tell my heart...

- why not *Today*?

We are no longer alone....

- we are now *Together* within

these *Words*...

...I have been creating words to express thoughts
of my *Love*; it is only you!

- I've been thinking about YOU every day;

... about us being separate and

.... wishing we were one - together again.

~ within this *Life*;

~ we are still together;

~ and for good reason.... we are AND always will be
Betrothed.

*Our life together will always be precious to me
because: it has always been you!*

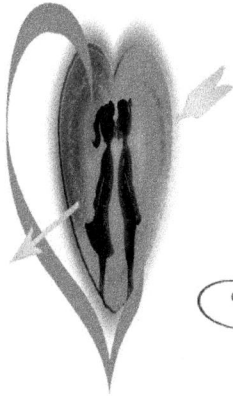

I wait for a sound:

....*Woken* by a dream.... where you laud my name
as a invocation;

....it drifted past your lips;

...a palpable tone - that cracked the sound of
emptiness;

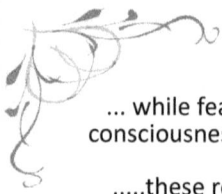

... while feathery *Intercourse* filled the abandon consciousness;

.....these reflections became the siren announcing;

.... you don't think of me this way *Anymore.*

Eternally:

... desire to re-kindle love-intoxicated *Teenage* frenzy;

Heart; ...ones that could warm this old man's

....inclined into a right of a sane mind;

...I'm a fool but;

.... what else can be voiced - that hasn't emerged between us;

....You were my favorite *Faux pas!*

I gave up hope, then gave up giving:

...as alone and barren as *Cinderella's* broom;

....when all you know or ... all you care about is gone;

.... all I know is what made WE evaporated;

... if I imagine too long; consciousness gave way to forgetting ... so I could heal;

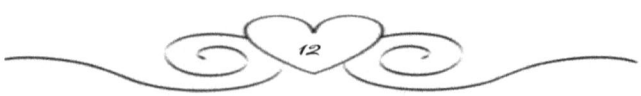

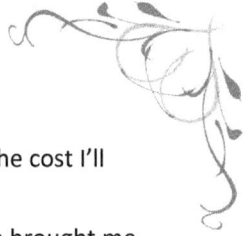

... maybe nothin' lasts forever.;

....to get YOU back...*Whatever* the cost I'll atone.

Long ago, inviting whispers would have brought me to beg;

...I've come a long way from there;

...have grown past days with you at my *Lap*;

...you have not been mine;

...even if we stayed together;

...would this glass be half full or half *Empty*?

OUR future is all but past us by...

...opening your heavenly gateway to me;

...I just need to hear your invitation so those gates swing open to me!

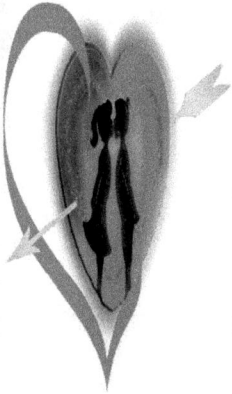

young love Again.....

oh, how I wish I had

Young Love again!

- for all the strife and ideas of NEW...

- I always thought; how could we always be us TWO...

- the world has had many $\mathcal{E}$mpress's but none more beautiful than YOU...

   - all the most gallant Princes in this world intently wished they were me so... they too might have a chance to be with YOU....

   - they all wanted to play this $\mathcal{C}$hivalous role so, hey might be simpatico.

- because I knew YOU would always be there, the sweetest sounds that YOU whispered to me was ADIEU.....

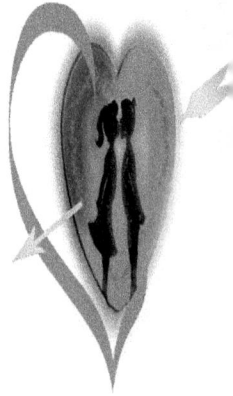

   - when I return we became ONE with legs snarled making ONE not TWO,

   - our private time together was always a work of art TOO,

      - maybe because everything we did; as ONE - was brand NEW...

- you were there through the $\mathcal{D}$ifficult and the SUBDUE....

   - the knowing you were always there, was comforting for me TOO,

- maybe it was for the thrill of something OVERDUE...

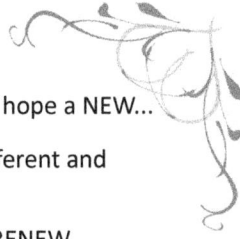

- maybe it was for the sweet feeling of hope a NEW...

- maybe it was for the desire of the different and NEW

- maybe it was for the *Promise* of RENEW....

- maybe for the constant ever-changing feeling that I KNEW ..

- because it was with YOU....

- I never faulted to love YOU....

- maybe because all that we did was for us TWO....

- maybe it is STILL the feeling of being with YOU....

**** I know now it was all ... because of YOU!

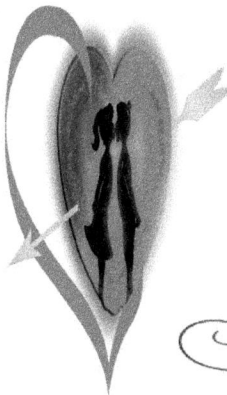

Hearts Asunder:

... sighs from the heart: murmur ~

.... no one hears...But me.

~ *Reflections* never shared;

....heartfelt intuition needs to be freed;

....*Words* can no longer open the recesses of my heart and,

.... bridge your conscience: because;

.... I now walk alone; *Searching.*

....they say you have to walk, not crawl.

~ my memories have become a pathway to our youth;

....where *Wise* men haven't found their way - past a point where I now find myself;

....I hang my head till fears disappear;

...I place my solemn face in your lap to caress;

....as I feel our shared warmth;

...these shadows of the past....

- guide me to thoughts of *Happiness!*

I'd love the idea of being close enough to see your longing smile;

...as long as I don't miss your *Whispers*: loss;

...no one ever speaks aloud - so no one ever lies: thoughts;

...all that is left is the *Sound* of *Loneliness*: exhale;

....it is the silence of castles walls: built around my heart - to protect this screaming essence:

Pounding;

....both; once in love, now just lost....

~ I know my head needs to silence my heart's anguish;

...wishing you were *Always* near so I can tell you this everyday: Alas...

.... to hail sympathies from character squandered;

....*Words* can set me free;

....my youth filled with unsure deeds - confronting an impaired mind;

...broken promises of "I do's" were followed by "I don't";

.....transpired and paralyzed by the silence of a romance gone;

- - all are seen through the *Window* of old age;
...where a love's sundown's are awash in shades of gray ash matching my heart as it escaped *Hell's* eternal grasp ~

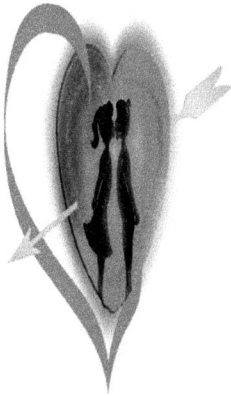

I lose sleep:

...Being a part of your life now has me dreaming of more....

Being a part of your life has me yearning for just a little more....

Even though my heart yearns for you to hold me, I yearn more to gather you up in my grasp, in a unending clutch, that never fades.

I dream of a girl that will hold my heart like it is a single _Vital_ rose out of an entire bouquet.

I hunger for a girl to spend Friday night on a couch .... full of _Cuddling_ together - mingling as one, rather than going to a club and being amongst a throng of strangers.

My heart goes to the girl who would wait on me hand and foot; as I slave away earning a living to keep her in comfort that would envelop those lovely hands in velvety gloves.

My _Heart_ is unburden by a woman that says we should stay at home and I'll make you your favorite dinner ... then going out to a fancy restaurant.

I would rather go to watch a _Seaside_ sunset to share secrets with you, then going to a movie premiere.

I would rather hold this woman's heart in my durable grasp, rather than holding her bags while she is shopping for unnecessary piece of jewelry.

This girl makes me smile as I *Dream* at night; someone that can make these dreams accentuated more than what WE are now.

I think.... so I love:

~ *I think nonstop about Yesterday's*

Love Today ~

- WHAT does true love look like and how does it look like on a man?

- HOW does it feel?

- WHY do some men never know.....

- Maybe I have found it in tomorrow's yesterday.

- I saw it in that face in the mirror... looking back on days gone by.

- Today I see that face again... in the hours of *Nowadays*...

... Could it be that my happiness ended yesterday? I THINK!

- I do know *Happiness* comes from a deep longing for love in one's heart.

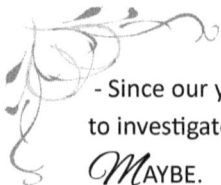

- Since our yesterdays; I haven't had opportunity to investigate myself .... WHAT, HOW, WHY and, *M*AYBE.

I have seen it before in other people's faces yet mine has been blank for years of Today's.

I need you more than Yesterday's *T*odays... filled with *P*romises of tomorrow!!!

Reconciliation:

I am reconciling my thoughts and *E*motions once; an hour ago- so happy, so full of promise; *N*ow self-loaveing.

.... I have been to the point of joy and hope - that I have never experienced before - only to be in distress an hour later, after reading what you wrote to me. *I welled up in tears.*

... I can't *R*econcile my thoughts:

.... I have been a fool and a bully. I am not proud of the fact that I have been a *M*onster.

... I have not known how much a monster until I see what I did to you through the eyes of a *F*ather...

.... I truly have to say *My* MIND was blank until we started talking; my mind was wiped clean of these and so many other events.

....To explain more is going to drive me *Crazy* AGAIN, it was a time that might have been hell to the normal male but to me after we broke up ....
I broke with *Reality*.

- It took months of *Healing* and conciliating that ... I would never wish upon my most hated enemy.

When I *Broke*, I broke *Totally*.

......a *Monster* because, the words that you used to described what I did shook me to my core. My not recalling ....is a symptom of my *Deep* dread.

I have been trying to deal with your words.

... For hours now ... I have been *Numb*, cloudy eyes and a mouth so dry I could hardly breathe, I am now in a state of *Depression*.

I can't help but not talk to you, I want to no longer bring you Pain.

I can't think about what I did to forget these things. I know now, I would never be able to *Live* with *Myself* after doing things like this to you.

I have been in despair since you told me about what I did and yet, you brushed it all aside to talk about happier things that happened between us.

My *Eyes* were welling up as they are right now as I am writing this.....I miss you but; can't let myself be the person that could do this again.

I went for a walk - with a broken heart. I fell to the ground and could not get back up. Some of the things that I repressed must have come up to be relived.

I can't tell you for how long I was there thinking about how I could have been such a bad person.

....it has been too *Painful*.

- I can't and won't ever be the same person;

- I can't and won't ever be able to talk to you as we just did a *Day* ago;

- I can't and won't ever *Forget* your forgiveness but, I now can't *NOW Forgive* myself;

- I can't and won't deny my *Seemingly* lifelong love for you;

- I can't, cant, can't ever deny that I thought we were *Moving* to a better place;

- I can't and won't *Ever* forget your love and the life that we tried to create together, the loss of that life, affects me now like it never would have in the past;

- I can't believe I have been in your life and looked so forward to continue our *Path* towards being together in a way I yet cannot understand.

- I can't believe how *Happy* you have made me, 30 years ago and again just a day ago.

- I can't believe I said I LOVE YOU!

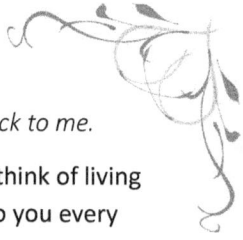

- - I can't believe *You* said it back to me.

- - - I can't believe and it is hard me to think of living *Without* being able to say it more to you every day.

- I can't believe now that I won't be able to see us looking back at each other in a mirror ten *Years* from now.

- I won't give up the fact that we could have been on that path but, I CAN'T ever see that happening now.

... Asking me why I am writing this as my eyes cloud up again, I tell myself that all the good things we had won't ever outweigh the Bad that I created.

Losing the life that we created was one reason your *Father* kept us apart but, if I was in his place I would have flat out told ME, that as your father - I can't let YOU do this ever to my daughter again.

... Your father was right to keep me from you, even as I write this I am regretting the words yet, the sadness I am experiencing now tell me that it is true, I never deserved such a person as you BE-CAUSE you gave me your whole heart and I obviously dismissed it.

I have with *Heavy* heart, wet face and a throat that is horse - without saying a word - that we should consider what we have done and say to ourselves; this is the definition of *Pain*.

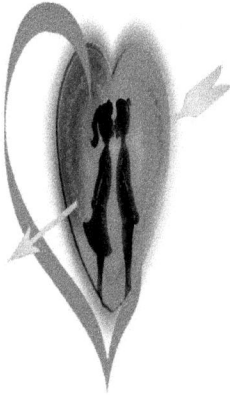

.....The Tragedy of LOVE:

Breakups are hard .....

They are supposed to be.....

- - Not a day goes by - -

- with glimpses into the past;

~ in *Reflection*....

..... a heart feels *Heavy* this relationship IS STILL unfinished;

...... it can drive you mad !!!

EVERYONE SAYS:

.... you need time to *Mourn*;

.... time heals all - *they say* and

eventually - you'll meet someone else.

- This has been said for all of human history;

....maybe; I can make you a distant memory;

...... *breakups happen,*

no matter what,

I cannot get over why I lost *YOU.*

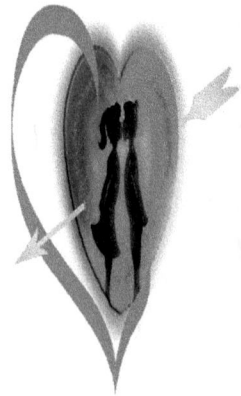

FORGETTING IS EASY?

That is;

- until that song;

   - seeing that *Photo* ~ the one that yearns to be shared;

   - wakening and still thinking of you ... *past the dreams*;

...then;

We are right back to square one.

  ~ Some people come in and out of your life....

  - this chapter has to end, my mind said;

   .....but, you can't quit 'em

    .... not ever my heart *Admits* to my brain;

   ..... I am thrust into love's *Purgatory;*

   - where the love of your life is waiting for you in your mind yet, *You aren't.*

   - - This purgatory is so magnetically seductive, it is my unyielding yearning;

   - - One's heart can't help but to constantly pulled back to this prediction;

   ..... this half of a *Soul* mate is biding time till we find one another;

      - - *Hanging on!*

    - - listening to music ... that reminds anyone that has been in this limbo - of being human;

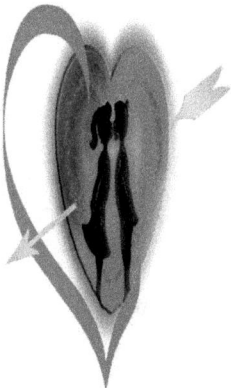

....when you know, you *Know*

- that connection that only comes around once; allowing one to keep holding on;

...... continually moving forward towards a past;

- holding onto heartfelt *Passion* has its own reasons....

.... of which reason knows nothing;

...... *as pain is Malicious.*

....some of us have to fight, breakup, makeup;

..maybe because, it is our heart's *Orchestration*!

Maybe you have to learn and grow.....

.... growing apart ~ *Resolves*;

- to finally know what is important;

- - before you can settle down with one soul forever;

.... until then we miserably sit in *love purgatory* hoping;

..... not to self-destruct.

.... mature *You* says; this isn't hard;

- your heart might *Say*:

"just because things were easy for you

- it doesn't mean they will be easier for your soul"

....*Love is Messy.*

BE-ing with You:

We'll not do anything at all....

*E*verything is going on around us.... without us because;

- separate from the world we are together .... alone!

....on your own;

... we are not complete;

- together we match like someone's *F*eet.

...We don't need anything, or anyone else;

- If we just stay here dammit;

...we can forget the *R*est of the planet;

.... we can be *O*ne and, the same;

- it is not what I think should happen, but it is the game.

I don't know how I can stay forever bound in your arms;

...let's make like we use to and not spoil the ending;

.... For days on end;

...let's *P*retend, that it will always be us two;

.... I never want to say *A*dieu;

- we will always moil to be together, without due.

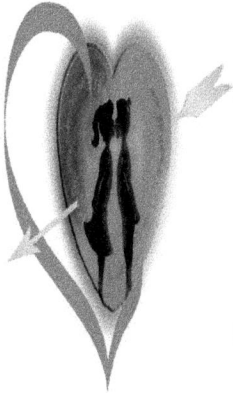

-- Let's say....

- let's forget what we have been told;

...let's get it right before we are too old;

.... let's make our lives *Whole*

....and;

- let's make our time together bold;

.....I want our souls to bloom;

~ like a Springtime romance that never gets old!

Those *Three* words...

- that we have spoken ... over and over through the years;

... are said much too little as of late;

.... much can be said for *Repetition* ... that does abate;

~ they are not enough to represent ..... what I really need to tell you again ....and *Again*;

Let's not waste time chasing dreams;

- we have been messing around dreaming in my head;

- us living separated - together for a lifetime;

- just like we were in different beds;

- safe and secure with our love *Guiding* us this time;

- I need to show you, there is a way!

I need your face, to remind me of a soul deep, in solitude...

- I need to *Seek* a resolution;

..... That finds a way into your life once again.....

Deep inside your heart;

....is the *Best* place to BE-gin.

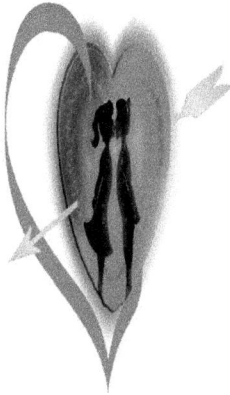

There has as never been a good time to say I am leaving....

your life was full nights of loneliness;
... married to my career;
- trepidations of saying good night to you troubled;
... I didn't really want to go;
- leaving your side I thought was a husband's duty;
... It called to me ... *Generations* deep;
- love of our togetherness ... my heart would steep;
...while we were away .... my heart does weep;

...then, we worked together ... I thought ....OUR
matrimony would keep.
 - After that attempt you said; it is time...
     ...."Now it is the time for us two to grow - justly"
      ....this was my time to admit .... I had to bid
YOU a bitter-sweet adieu;
      ....I wanted..YOU needed....but respectively WE
do.
  ...better times remembered:
   - I want to take in all of YOU;
      ....from your pictures ... so happy and not blue;
    ...a time when your youth was keep us in sync and
feeling new;
  ...drinking a cheer to yesterday's filled with US two;
 .... my life would not have turned out the same if it
wasn't for YOU!

...*One* day at a time:
 - ONE at time; trying to make do...
   .... I thought maybe I can drink away memories of
YOU;
     ...that whisper that lingered in my soul says...
       ..... you might as well try to steal rain from a
cloud;
 ..... you will come away with the same bottomless
empty flask.

 - So I convince myself....don't let go to what you
held dear;

                Year after year;
   ..... the depths of my soul hears;
  .....drum beats deep within...it begs for repair;
 ...my head says NO but, my heart says: hold on tight;

 'Cause I'm on my way back to you tonight!

The day after you Left me:

*....I thought my life was working ... to give you
treasures bought - but, then it was not.....*

I Lost it all....

-- I didn't acknowledge the why,

---- I came to know....

....*YOU* made me *alive*.

Now I am dead....

-- lying here in an empty bed; thinking.....

YOU have given me a *Life*; undeserving of your grace;

....more than its seemingly *Rife* with worthlessness;

- that stagnates now in this room.

Why shouldn't I try to fix our relationship...

I mucked up?

S- all I want to do; is lie here and die in my own *Sorrow*.

It has already been *Two* days - not a movement;

- my bed became my *Grave*;

- all I can do is think;

- - about what I'd be without you;

....*Nothingness*.

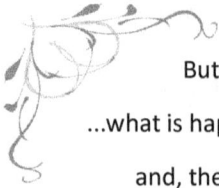

But all I need is a chance to explain;

...what is happening in my *Head*

and, then try to understand why we parted;

as the *Pain* in my heart grows.

I think we have seen each other

at our most Vulnerable....

....needing to save these memory's and the ones of what makes you happy ... over the things that makes you sad ... are etched in my *Memory*:

....what were your dreams and desires?

....what were your *Passions*? ... what made you happy?

.....I wanted to touch you, without touching you skin, deep into your heart through my words, earning your love through my deeds.

~ *Before* SHE leaves for good;

...this chance to talk through the turmoil;

- *Why* is this happening?

- - how did WE get to this point?

.. *Could I have turned this it around ?*

....I need to come to an agreement with myself to be a better *Man*;

... all the while hoping SHE won't turn me down;

-all I want to do Is hold her tight;

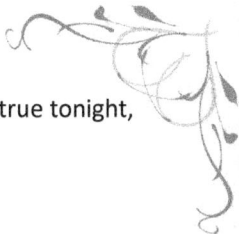

- - - and make our dreams *Come* true tonight,

Once and for all....

- I know I can make her happy;

.... instead of the screaming, yelling,

...making life sorrowful.

I feel that saying Sorry ... will never be enough

to take away the pain.

- I'm not asking for a brand new start;

... I want this to be a part of our life;

....our *Past*,

- so we know to not let it happen again.

You were my *Entire* life.

- Without *YOU,* I became nothing;

- - Why didn't we give it another chance?

- - - was it that bad?

- - - - that trying was too remote?

We could have made it into something.

- I love you too much to say;

- - I should have, could have and would have....
Done - so much *More*.

Now, I can't let you go....

....*Look* into my eyes, so I can say:

I love you

~ I do .... !

... A
Beginning

Your Soul's on Fire

"She scares you a little.
Good she should" .....

- You are complicated and that is the way it supposed to be;

- You make me fear love because it is serious making two people one;

- I have been lucky enough to be a part of your life, enjoying the surprising strength of your convictions;

- You bring beauty with this strength, as others take notice that this beauty is yours alone;

- It is all encompassing and is felt all around you;

- It pulses through your veins as your soul is beauty itself.

Never take this Soul for granted:

- You are fierce as soulful;

-Loving you could be unruly and this love can take my soul on a tour of heaven or hell;

- Reining in this soul can unleash a burning love within our fused veins;

- An arising internal storm streaking through my body has created my fervor for life;

- My love amidst it all is cherished as it was significant;

- Your face, *Beauty* personified, shows that soul every time it is seem by me.

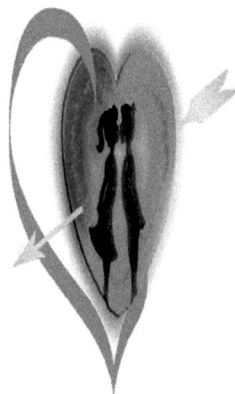

Forever loves forevermore

_I don't know when Your whispers awoken
My love, but My heart is captivated...._

When I say I love You,

I don't mean I love You more;

... more than the bad days;

... more than after any fight we had;

... more than the miles are between us;

... more than any obstacle that might keep us
Detached;

... more than the sun radiates even on our _Moony_
and austere days;

... more than the stars light up the sky without Your
moon.

If a man Loves You;

He craves You....

He desires Your touch...

He yearns to hear the sound of Your voice, then;

He leans in closer to hear Your whispers;

....hearing our hearts beat louder as one;

...it is made clear, _Your_ heart belongs to Him.

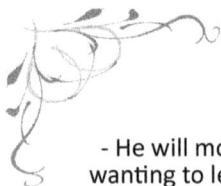

He will make...

- He will move *Mountains* to be with You, never wanting to leave his place besides You.

- He will call You, wanting just to make a connection.

-He will text *You*, because writing words take more thoughtfulness.

-He will remind You of how important you are too him, by never saying goodbye first.

-He will call You beautiful instead of pretty, always saying that Your beauty will always be in his memories.

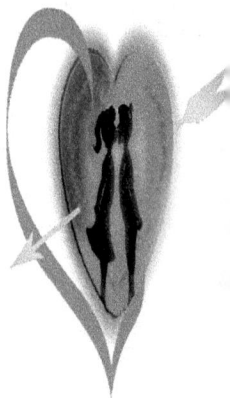

-He will remind You how sexy You are by suggesting revealing things that You should wear only for Him.

-He will tell You all the time You are His world and His thoughts always revolve around Your universe.

-He will show You ... these things while His heart beats ... out of His chest when ... You are near.

Let Me lose Myself in You....

Forevermore...!

<u>Those Eyes:</u>

I wonder why;

...why do they lie?

...they were here for me to *Gaze* into forever;

...now I endeavor, to not fall in love again.

I am dying to ask;

...what do you think?

...do your eyes think of a task;

...before they make my heart sink?

your eyes are on fire;

....my mind is ablaze;

....falling again for that gaze;

...it has been just in time;

...we have always in the right place;

...I never wanted a woman more;

...one that is not *Commonplace*;

...yours is the face ... I desire;

...I never thought it could be evermore;

... but, those Eyes

... they still set my heart on Fire.

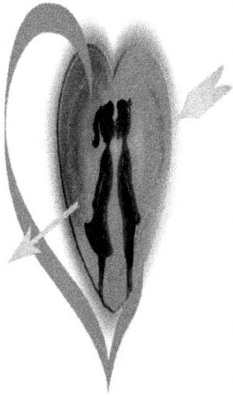

Your Facets:

....are perfect for the man who

wants to Love you....

....not being there throughout the years has been the hardest things ever vindicated and is still NOT worthy of every faded scar on my memory of us.

...you leaving was the deepest Scare I still have; finding you again is perfect rapturous agony. I'd still rather be there ... in my sullen mind ... than anyplace else in the world.

....the promise of your love Embraces like a voluminous robe flowering with a soul-deep love that makes my pulse quicken with eventuate hope.

...Visions of you are always in my waking hours, still wishing for the time that it won't be a vision but your face that I see when I wake.

.... I know the makeup rule in the morning yet; still I want to see you and you waking up beside me.

....What you consider an imperfect presence is my ideal dream; one that started 30 years ago and still deep within my heart - it is still raging today !

Memories answer my dreams...

Your face beams;

....in my dreams!

Memory Economics;

    ....one memory shared - can make two people happy!

    ..... my fading memories are stories of heartbreak and happiness!

Memory Onus:

....take my hand and show me how to keep you by my side forever;

    ....I don't wanna let it go;

    ....that would be the best for the rest...it is therapy for me;

    ....my waking breath - at sunrise;

    ...seems to bring me YOU;

    ....every sunset too!

Memories of YOU;

    ....bring to mind memories we once knew;

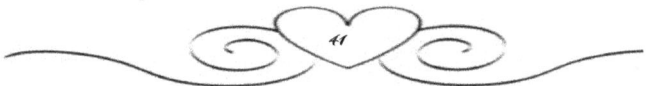

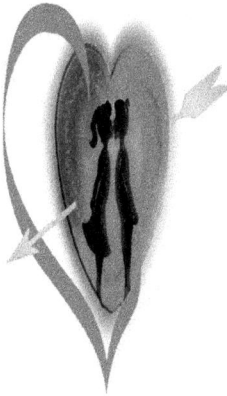

...here and there - *Everywhere*;

...recalling times with YOU.

Waking my up to your footsteps leaving our *Bed*;

.....make a sound that still dawdles in my head;

....a melody so hard to dwell upon;

....I drape a pillow instead.

what gets me through the day;

....is the thought of us *Forever;*

....I hope it is the one that won't ever go away!

All I need to know is;

...where to stop to listen to your *Heartfelt* songs;

...that I want to write down every letter;

....to every word you ever sang.

So let's hold to these together;

....memories after all gave me hope;

....I never want to say I've got to let *Go*.

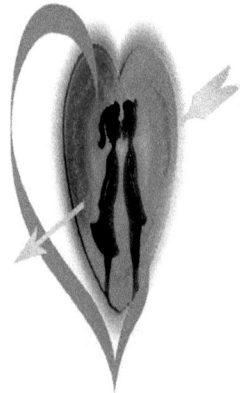

WE wrote our story;

 ....WE sang our songs;

  ....WE hung our memories like *Trophies* on a wall;

   ....you answered my devotions;

   ...these cherished moments are carved in OUR stone;

   .... never will I ever let them go!

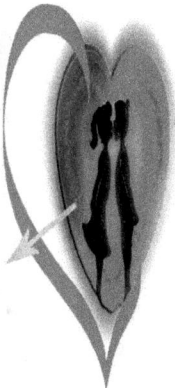

What is the meaning of life?

 ....relationship memories that should have been as important to you as they were to that someone special.

Revisiting a past love:

 ...when re-accounting memories of WE;

  ....WE finally realize how important YOU were in MY life.

Memories are *Unforgotten* as some are forgiven:

 ...once found again - through another's eyes - you realize the importance you played in their life;

  ....forgotten but once re-lived makes your life complete;

.... in spite of everything I do;

....and every way I tried to forget US;

....memories seem to return;

ME to YOU

Today I caught Myself smiling:

.... for no reason at all - then, I finally figured it out; it is because of you.

...you have had an Effect on me!

...Every morning I look forward to opening notes from you.

..... I have been Affected by you.

... All my spare time is looking for words to tell you more about my life and my dreams of YOU.

... you have infected my Soul.

 - I see your face in everything I read to or an adventitious thought.

... I have been Affected by you.

- I see happy couples all day and it makes me stop and wonder what it would be like .... with you.

... why has this affection *Effected* my everything?

- Today even the skies seem bluer with you in my life... it has been effected in a way I didn't see coming.

.....when will I be certain if this *Affection* be permanent?

You have effectively changed the way I look at the world and our place in it.

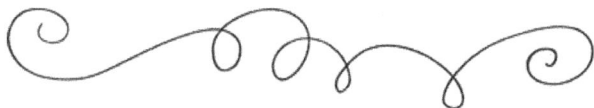

The First Spark:

Just being near you was taking away my control over breathing;

....you became my natural high;

- every *Breath* was a *Whirlwind* of emotions:

-- that filled my body like a *Hurricane.*

- I can feel the strength of my desires build;

....they were as persuasive as a drug;

... my mind is flying;

- - being in the same room made my heart pound like a *Vivaldi* stanza;

...as my skin will start to sweat.

- My soul has connected without a touch;

by the time I realized we were one;

- I was thinking about how...

How I fell so quick under your *Spell*?

......How did I fall for a friend's sister?

- What was this leading to?

.....It was too late to ask;

....I was already *Spellbound*.

The first *Kiss* I can't remember but,

.... I do know all the kisses sent me to the *Alter*.

- I know that not only did the first one make my heart open....they became my addiction.

My heart beat for you and no other!

.... Your smiles made time stand still;

- all your *Smiles* have made my life feel like my heart was never detached from your spirit.

...I always hear your voice; it is a slight whisper to my heart;

- I feel you in my dreams, to my waking twilight.

.....You are always with me!

~ I had become *Addicted* to your touch; your lips, your fingers, your body; when they met, I thrived;

- my heart swells and lungs sing out with sighs of fulfillment.

...I have never craved another's Touch as I have yours!

I want to lose my inner self doubts as I gaze deep within you...

- Your soul opens to me more, I lose myself more;

So no one will see Me ... without seeing that you have always been my first!!!!

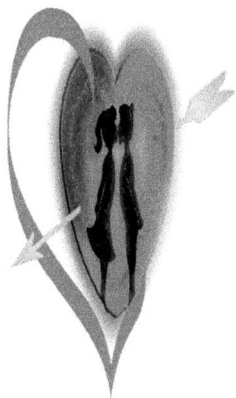

To love is to truly be Alive:

I have stayed silent too long;

... after this silence, my heart can no longer be harnessed.

... *Asking* myself why I have love - no longer?

.... is it me or is it my selfishness halting me to be in a headstrong love affair?

I ask myself to look into my unruly heart; *Why?*

... because when I had *Love* like this; I was too *Mulish* to understand the other side of a perspective;

... thinking twice before reserving a space in my heart;

... to hold it from fluttering away unrestrained with a promise of wining your love;

- I exercise my right to grasp yours....

... as hearts race, I see reassurance from you;

... a pulse that was once still, has *Awoken* with you now in my arms...

....I Know that I am truly alive once again!

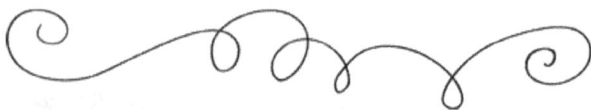

I am without YOU...

standin' in the dark;

....on this bridge between what is known and unknown;

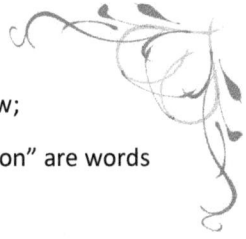

...I thought I'd find you here by now;

    ..."maybe", "sometime" and "soon" are words that linger.

There is *Rain*;

  ...it is as long as a month of days;

    ....my footsteps have been washed away;

    ...I can't find my way back to YOU;

    ...memories are gone;

    ....a storm of tears has washed them from my life.

Everything is a mess;

  ...MY face is willowed;

    ....I am still looking for that place;

    ....where I can find that space;

    .... where MY heart was blessed.

Yet Again, I am still standing

on a bridge alone.

I'm searching for a myth;

  ...one that began with me,

    .....grew into we and;

..... is again I alone.

- Is there anybody I know here .... everything so confusing;

.....nothing is going steadfast;

....no one wants to be adrift without an anchor;

.....maybe,

....MY mind needs to barren;

....so it can inheriting new serenity.

Take the lead, so I can make our way back to WE;

....*Somewhere* new, something to see;

......I don't know who WE are;

....But, I'm with YOU!

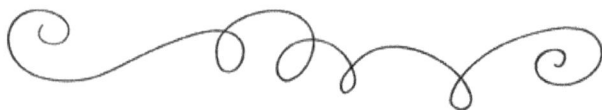

what it was like Without you:

...*Without* you there, I sit heavy hearted,

just *Being*....

... a part of nothing; alone and not alone;

Feelings Felt:

...with every sad love song that played on the radio... is *Misery* now my life?

...hurt, confused, feeling *Neglected* all at once, made it hard just to breathe let alone live like a "*normal*" man;

...when you feel pain you Know you're alive, so I Smile;

..it is okay people say, this is what it suppose to be like;

...no one ever told me that Being

dead inside would feel so normal;

...it's okay to feel this way I thought ... that is what everyone says ... so I mandated my mind to *Forgetfulness.*

...this doesn't change the fact that you are gone, out of my life like an *Exhale*;

...I didn't know it was going to be 30 years till I'd be able to draw another breath.

...I understand now.

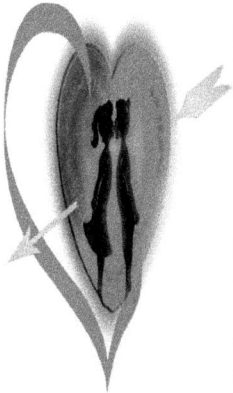

If I could Change Things:

In the Past....

It's was like;

- She doesn't hear the words I meant to say;

....is her mind somewhere far away or in-between;

- another relationship;

- is she way too serious.

.....You and I;

- We were face to face but,

... you couldn't hear what I want to say;

- *I was thinking this and ... you that.*

Like Water and the Stone...

- *I could never stay mad at you because water eventually wears away the stone.*

- We were Venus and Mars;

...we are now as different as the Stars;

- our hearts were in harmony like every love song ever sung;

- - I wouldn't have changed a thing.

- - my past feelings....

- I never want to change;

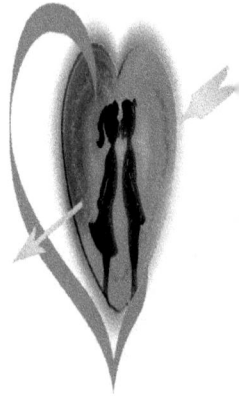

- - like *Fire* and *Rain;*

- - - you can drive me insane;

... no, I cannot change.

*I want to see you in my dreams every night because
now, I never see you face to face.*

I want to Feel you in my dreams because

there, I can't hold your cheeks and kiss your face.

...Even in my dreams;

- we are different;

- - I want to hold you like never before;

and you always say;

- maybe someday soon.

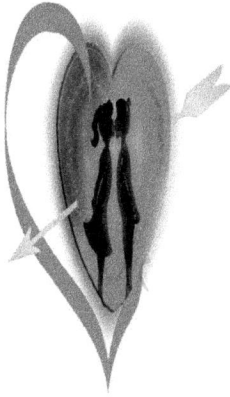

If it was up to Me...

us two....

would already be We!

the moment....of We:

the moment our lips touched

the First time...

~ memories were made and kept ~

Memories of that night escape but it was this night that kept me coming back to you.... with abandon;

....WE kept looking forward to our next encounter;

....WE kept looking for every opportunity to make WE a permanent branding;

....WE took every moment ... to become a single identity;

....WE loved to be together at all costs;

....WE needed to make each other the object of desire;

....WE didn't look for another because, we already found our NUMBER ONE's;

....WE became books, ready to read and became the most beautiful love story written;

....WE became each other's daydream love;

....WE found what made us cry and try to become More;

....WE found what made us smile to become
        ---- more like One;

....WE found each other's serious spots, that let us know each other in a way only *Lovers* do;

....WE loved the naughty and the nice;

....WE touched and mingled our lips, fingers, hands and legs to become ONE;

....WE knew right from wrong and wrong became the fun things we did;

....WE made mornings as romantic as our nightly *Tryst*;

....WE learned how two divergent thoughts and souls could merge;

....WE could inter-fuse our taste for each other ... your skin next to mine, the taste of you on my lips as the scent of last night's *Passion* filled the room;

....WE strive for togetherness;

....WE found out how to be comfortable ... telling stories;

.....WE learned deep *DESIRES* that brought me close as a moth can come to your *FLAME*;

....WE knew what it was like to desire lives filled with kisses, sex and, all-night long after-sex *Embraces*;

....WE felt like we have been as one forever and now knew what the other felt;

....WE found no shame in knowing what each one of us wanted from the other;

....WE didn't have to pretend again;

....WE needed to belong to each other;

....WE strive for *Forever*;

....WE didn't look far enough into the future to see us become *We* again;

....WE should strive again for WE;

....WE should wake together so I can say good morning beautiful;

....WE should look to the *US*, in *OUR* past *WE's* and;

    ....I want you to think about missing my *kiss*, *touch* and *love*; as much as I miss yours.

Life is what WE have
let it Become:

...after you said we needed a *Break*,

....the break never *Ended*.

.....I was lost in the *Questions*...

- *What*?

- *How*?

- Is this *Real*?

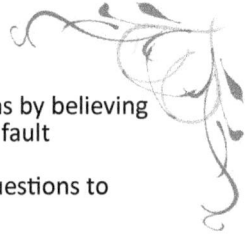

I could have ended my reflections by believing no, it is not Me, it's the other person's fault

....yet there are *Always* more questions to answer.

- Looking for a way;

- to be your *Man* again;

- Maybe not the next day;

- just looking for any way;

-- *Maybe* not now, maybe not in a day....

- - - or *Two*;

.....'Cause nothing gonna *Evolve*;

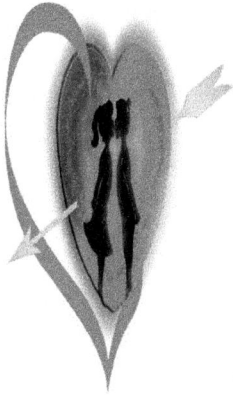

- If WE stay here in this *Rut*;

....'*Cause* I am trying to resolve to

- live a *Simple* life but;

.... I can't, 'Cause I'm *Involved* in the world of prestige and.... Elegance;

- my mind says live simpler - *Don't* have such apprehensions...

... while you live with a *Vengeance*!

.... in the life that chose *ME*;

- I cannot do what is conventional;

- there are too many assumed expectations;

- that are demanded by who have *Sociable* speculations;

- I am the one who loves to break all the rules....

... this is who I have *Become.*

******

...WE've gotta do what it takes *TWO* - to fix:

....what TWO bungled.

... to say: I will *Fix* this - isn't the easiest answer;

... even if you think that it isn't necessary;

.......it's all in our hands how WE handle the rest of our lives.

...it is up to *How* open *WE* are to *Admitting* there is a way out.

- WE can say I made mistakes;

... WE made mistakes;

-- it's never too late to think again;

--- why don't WE fix *US*?

*****

Take a *Breath* says my soul;

.....and say a invocation;

...with the *Right* woman's love

- couples that fall in *Love* come with memories of oneness...

....take your *Mind* away from here;

.... anywhere, but right here;

- *R*ight now...

....our hopes and dreams are out *T*here;

- somewhere WE will find the love that we crave.

* * * * * *

Don't let WE pass by because;

- of what someone else told US on how WE should live;

... because WHO they are and where they come from;

- - If this life gets any harder;

.... WE won't let nothing or NO one keep *U*s down;

... WE should just be WE.

...... Maybe YOU and I shouldn't have said good-bye;

- to our hopes and dreams;

- that are still there just *B*eyond OUR view from this place;

....it has become plain to see when my eyes are wide shut.

.... don't let these reconcile times pass;

- this time is something you can never get back;

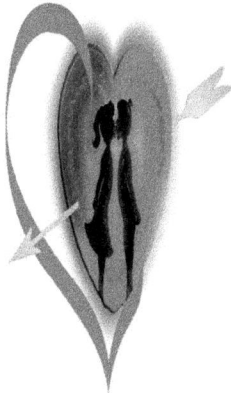

- - because people come and people go;

- - - And then sometimes come back again;

We'll just keep moving onward to a better day;

....I see a bluer skies in MY life;

- *Because*, you were there with ME once and maybe again...

....You could have a better life NOW with someone;

~ Open your eyes and you might see the same *Boy* has now become that *Man* you tried to build;

- this is where US will be no more. ... it was never ... ever meant be the same.

....you aren't;

....we aren't;

......those *Young* kids.... won't ever either.

No one can stop US from being WE in my mind;

- they will try but, WE won't let *Them*.

Memories are Forgotten as they were Forgiven:

...after all these *Years*....

.....do we *Really* care.

- It is not till we were parted that I knew how much you meant to me -

-- Hold on, I need to take you *Back* there....

- She said;

- Everybody needs a little alone time,

.... even the best of friends need to have space to grow time.

In my *Mind*.....

I shrieked ....

....all I need now is you to hold!

I couldn't stand being kept away;

.....even for a day.

- I forsaken my competence and my heart told me to do the impossible;

....get you back in my arms again;

to say; "I know - *Sorry* - can't fix us,"

.....It has always been hard for me to say I am *Sorry*.

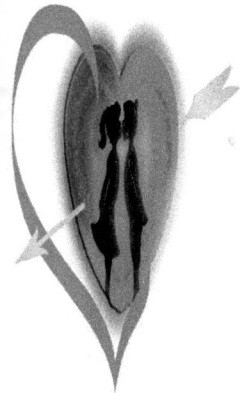

~ I needed you to be by my side,

I want you to Stay ~

.... these words detached from my soul without you hearing them from my *Lips*;

...only thing heard was the *Shattering* screams of silence - of a too *Proud* heart holding true.

Again...

....Being able to *Reconcile* all that we've been through....

- to promise it would only get better;

- - is my *Plight*.

...Compelling me to eternally think of *US*.

~ I want to be Swept away ~

.....to a place of peace;

..... a place not far away from the *One* that I *Love*.

......You're the part of me I just can't let go!

~ You were the Lucky one ~

-- When I thought of you being gone;

...my whole world *Quaked*;

...my heart quickened to know I'd might unexpectedly catch a glimpse of you.

-- When *You* were gone;

.... my *World*, our world ceased;

.....no one will see us at these cross roads again, because now there is nobody there;

....The *Scattered* remnants of my heart were locked away to never be thought of again;

...It was like my Memories

vanished - to save my soul - from

the persecution of you

not being there.

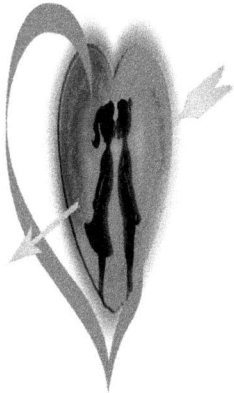

A future alone....in my mind:

Like an Unsure boy with a crush, I feel as though I am having the same happen to me now after rekindled love is appearing jostled....

Without being able to see the apprehensiveness developing on your face, gaze breathlessly into your eyes and then listening to your heart's converging joy from your hushed whispers; I feel

Unsure like a boy with an uninvited crush.

I feel as though responses from a love once in my *Grasp*, is now being a written off as a downplayed future. It is a monster in my head. Like a crazed clown character in a Steven King story, my mind.... undeniably weird for us to imagine yet, there every day.

Mentions of commitment to a *Relation-ship* are excused in brevity of words rendered like; maybe someday.

Overlooking comments of love, love-bites and lust; they are being dismissed peremptorily....

...maybe I have gone in a direction that could not been appreciated by my most desired love?

What is this sullen *Monster* in my head...

My interpretation of these responses; from a once devoted young love are now being pushed off as common or; an ordinary dated relationship.

What have I done to degenerate a beautiful *Charade* in my mind? Now it is time to generate my happy facade shields, one that protects my feelings so they can't be destroyed again.

- *Eminently* like a boyhood crush... It is all encompassing.

......Remembrances of daily tryst in young lust, shattered...

....Tender, whimsical loving snipes have been replaced by promises of some day and maybe soon.

My Feeling of desperation grows ... when I cannot directly talk to you.

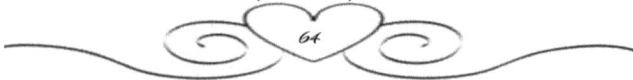

Older and wiser comments are being made instead of her heart-on-a-string and less than hurried *Quips*.

Daily despair has replaced daily joy and looking towards a brighter future has all but vanished.

Fantasies of it I *Dream* but, now are being replaced by; why we can't make dreams come true? Because, so many others are counting on us to do right by them.

Feeling of hopefulness is been replaced

by *H*opelessness in our *F*uture.

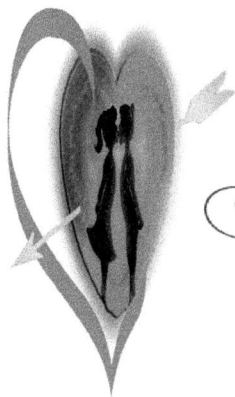

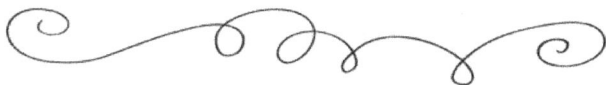

Without any Words from You;

my voice was stifled;

...What else did you expect me to do?

...I couldn't live without you.

~ It is a feeling of having unsubstantiated pleas

....that create my hopeless joy - from the fact that we

are talking once again ~

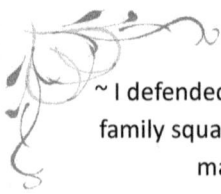

~ I defended you through the break up and the family squabbles; as if I had anything left to prove, I made out alive but, dead inside ~

After all that I've seen -

.....I always love the time when my *Eyes* are closed;

....in my *Dreams* I relive the happy times of US;

.....I know I have to *Un-love* you yet, don't want to.

....It is like the pride of winning the *World* Series in your dreams, all to have it end when you *Awake*.

....Sooner or later because it is just a happy thought, you know it has to end.

......Thoughts of you are happy in my mind, never wanting them to stop. This is the life I lead everyday with *You* in my dreams.

I got tired of feeling out of touch, so I reached out more often;
...I never felt more a part of your life - like I have in the last few months.
~ at times I've treated my bed like it was a tomb ~

.....now I *Wake* up excited after dreaming of you;

...... you've mystified me, I know I must *Defy* you by telling you how much I have thought about **US**;

..... if I hadn't *Loved* you for these dreams, I surely would *Hate* you for being there and *Not* be *Available*.

...when WE are near:

- You have the ability to read people better than others might care to. Strength and insight evolves from what you feel.....protective, compassionate and genuine.

... I love *Strong* women but know that your tenderness and capacity to love is what you protect - more than anything else.

...*Because* you give your whole heart you don't want to have false love so, you are very protective of your showing your feelings to anyone.

You may act *Shy* or *withdrawn ... as a protective device. I want to be close enough to Whisper in your ear how sexy I think you are and I want you to be able to freely tell me how Delighted that made you.*

....I love the way your body flirts with my mind.....my *BUNDA!*

...My *Blood rages as our Souls close.*
I want you to say to you - with a smile; my contentment is thinking about your touch. I want to say how sexy you are but, want you to know that your beauty is flowing over me. I'd like to be the gentleman that says how beautiful you are but, I would rather remind you with *Hours* of my undivided attention to satisfying that spot between your thighs.

- - - Alone time is necessary. A man is as good as he has to be to make his *Woman* be as bad she dares to be.
I want to free you of your concerns of self-protection by telling you what I think.

Chapter Two:

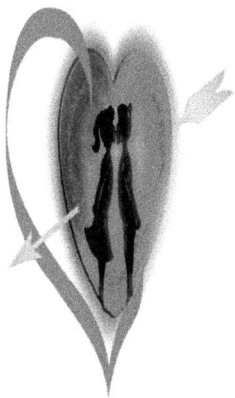

Cherishing
Love

Memories of the past Haunt my Heart like the hushed Voice of a Lover:

~ they brought me to think of a

Girl ... I used to know!

~ now that she is gone; Silence!

~ this roar of silence has become my Soul's

contentment ~

~ After you said **WE** were no more...

...my silence rose like Indivisible and sequester castle walls;

- it became the sound that Darkness makes without listening;

... as it became familiar as an Old friend;

- my Sympathies are Imprisoned in the idolize whispers of my soul.

~ They have become:

- the Restless dreams where I always now walk alone;

- the Rage shouting inside my heart;

... are my words falling like Frenzied rain;

- forming rivers of saddening Wretchedness;

- that becomes a river that cuts stone

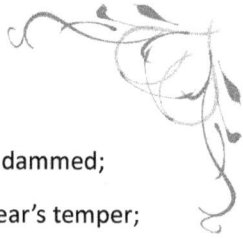

...with my ever present outpouring;

- that was once as *Cold* as the dammed;

...this anguish was never from fear's temper;

~ this river has dispelled the *Stone* of my heart.

The course of the river accommodates the hardness of the stone but;

- the *River still flows;*

.....as it has *Hollowed* the *Stone;*

- this river with its *10,000* voices;

.... it *Scribe* it's own songs of past course changes;

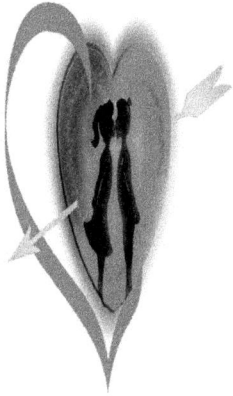

- that tell a story of an *Eon's* of joyousness gone by;

..... like songs of when **WE** were **ONE** but not alone.

~ Our *River* has turned a mountain of granite to a quarry of *Pebbles* ~

~ It is the naked light in our *Darkness*, that thunder bolts of Hope's *Neon*-light burst through the isolation that enshroud this quarry;

- it is the *Memories* of US that amplified these strikes.

****

~ *My Pleas*:

- become a single prayer; that scream towards *God's* ear;

.....we need to talk ....without speaking;

- why do my *Visions* creepily haunt me so;

.... telling of a love that was *Once* invincibly held by both;

- *"till death"* was never an unwelcome oath;

..... are now scant voices never heard by those that aren't there;

~ I await the words that *Heal* ME ~

My 'Shine:

I would sell my soul to be with HER

for one more stand...

....a dance with my *Queen* ... will be at hand; music flows....

....soothing the soul in my heart's homeland; racing to start...

.... WE will be dancing in between a *Sea* of covers; feels so right....

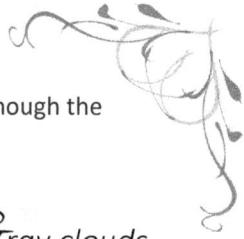

......WE grind through sunset, right though the dark; till morning light....

....'Cause you're my light.

.....*pushing through a* $\mathcal{G}$*ray clouds*

of haze;

....I took a stroll in your park; I was in a daze....

....i met an old friend there and; SHE felt so right...

....i didn't need gloomy shadows from the past; forever in my mind....

.......until the sun comes up again; strolling with a lover...

....one night was just too fast.

......HER love was one I could not ignore; biting my lip....

.... SHE knows what I adore; touch so soft...

.....what kind of trouble are WE in for; tomorrow will tell....

......it is my kinda like tugging at Hell's heartstring; still more...

....and I got mine during this tour; another trip to fantasy...

....cause I want more....

I was wishing...soon to pass:

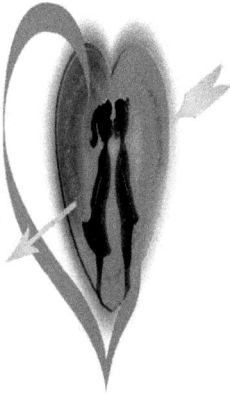

.....we had a divine fate that set us free; at last....

.....this tale ain't gotta do ME; unless....

.....just like the sunshine that breaks the morning dark; we ARE together....

.....*Evermore* and forever by my side; desire;

.......*OUR 'Shine is gonna let us see !*

Solace of loving you:

.....each morning the light leaks

through my bedroom windows

but, it's Brightness enlightens

that you are no longer there.

....the spot that is now empty, days earlier were filled with *Joy*;

....remembrances of a time *Less* stressful, filled with heaving pants driven by passion;

....I could no longer hold you close,

....I forced myself to **forget**, *forget*, forget.

******

My Mind is now filled with....*Solace*!

...thoughts of holding you close bring Solace;

...*Now* to be with you will bring Solace;

...my *Cherished* love renewed by glimmers of Solace,

...an embrace from you unfolds my heart's Solace,

...intertwined with *Your* smile, warmed by the calm after this *Storm* that became *Inescapable*; *You* are the *SOLACE* that brings me home.

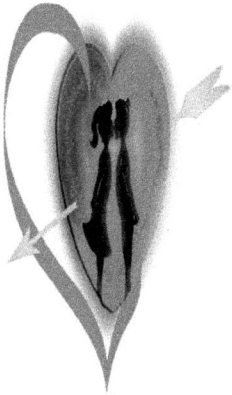

I wait:

I wait for the one that fills me with *Laughter*, one that can make me *Laugh* no matter my *Mood*;

I *Wait* for the one that even when I am mad... I want to *Work* it out with her;

I *wait* because you have lite a *Fire* in my *Soul*; one that is not tame and you know IT can't be with you.

..... *I wait* because IT needs to run *Free*;

.... *I wait* for you because you fulfill IT ... unlike others that can only take;

.... I *Wait* for you to fill IT with love;

... *I wait* because IT *Can't* accept less;

... *I wait* because IT deserves a *True* love, one that has lasted for years and years to come! ... *I wait for You!*

Love is cold:

Do YOU understand why the

Thirst of love feels Joyless?

What we have said...

   - to each other makes me think;

      - I need to again have the chance to warm your *Heart* unless;

..you decide I am not really the ONE;

...then you can just turn and run

but, on this plane;

.....once you get past our memories of *Omission* and pain again;

....we see our love can soar like Eagles wings...

-- You might learn...

to find your love for me once again;

a tiny bit of my heart's *Hope* still sings.

So swing...

....your heart open for me to try to *Win* your LOVE again...

...because love always finds a way to *Sting*.

We all feel a need to change and try the green grass on the other side that fence.

I need to *Rearrange*...

... my life to include a fondness that was long lost, moving on to a newly re-found love;

...the one that never got tossed;

... an enduring desire that has *BEGUN*;

... again that pours from my heart with a shout:

I SHOULDN'T POUT,

-- I need to be with my number ONE --

My dreams *Feel,*

as though they are already apart of a desire;

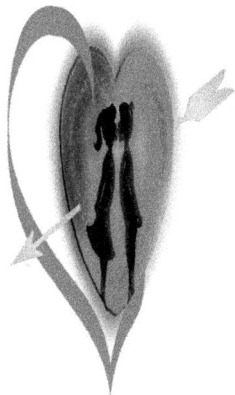

.... a desire for you to jump start my *Heart.*

.....a simple word; or a twisted thought can make me *Think* you....

-- *Show me how to*

restart YOUR Heart.

... a loving look or glance could make my heart *Pitter-patter* and *Dance.*

.... But if you are afraid to be true to an enduring love;

-- maybe we shouldn't take the chance.

Tell *Me;* am I hot or cold?

my Thoughts:

..... I tried not to think about them but,

the Silence was killing me!

~ I have realized what it is like to have an un-quenchable *Thirst* for someone;

.... I feel you in my dreams and nothing else moves me the way you have;

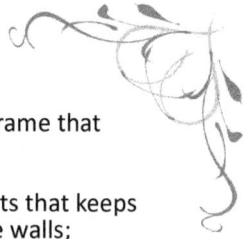

- *Marriage* is how we decorate a frame that hangs on our walls;

- - Love is how we gift wrap our hearts that keeps the world from breaking through these walls;

- - - since being wrapped up with you ... I have never *Craved* another, the same;

... the world now seems less important.

- I can't believe I had that girl in my *Arms*;

...the *ONE* I carried to bed after a day of toil.

.....the distance of time hasn't changed how I think of that girl - who became my *Poetry* .....while the rest of the world couldn't sing the alphabet on MTV.

~ You might have fallen in *Love* with a *bandit* smile or a *Unexpected* naughty laugh. It is OK to let your guard down and let your number *One* in without regrets....

... You respect him for his brain or power of will;

... if you dive a little deeper you'll find his heart that is Entrenched in love lost...!

~ She became my *Saint*, that made our lips sin ... with kisses that grasped my heart like the *Devil*;

.. as my lungs gasp for air because, making love to my *Number* ONE was as enthusiastic .... as beautifully *Exhausting*.

... you are biting my *Lip*;

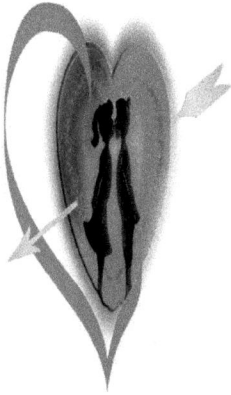

.....gripping the bed to control the shaking;

.....the overflowing *Sounds* of love in the room with;

....the occasional scream that occasionally leaked out ... was *Music* to my ears .... driving me to transcend with a smile that ... *ONLY* you know.

... *Afterwards* this exchange became so deep; so intense; so powerful that my mind felt as naked and fulfilled as our bodies;

.....every time I hear "*Hi ... Handsome*"!

.....How I yearn to feel your *Heart* pound against my *Chest*.

~ *Your smile is Breathtaking, the look in your eyes intoxicating.... I lose myself* ~

... because, now it doesn't matter where we end up, it is okay to be *Yourself*;

..... we started in each other's arms and ONLY YOU will *Forever* be my number ONE.

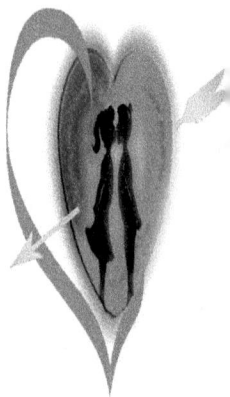

Our imminent spirits are now as Entangled as the lives that we live.

....without you, WHY?

Waitin' for you....

I can't find my Way;

...this isn't the end, just the *Journey* leading to WHY!

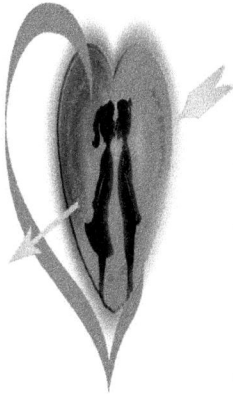

.....momma says, "it is *Gonna* take a little time";

......to mend your *Overcome* heart;

- *Love* is all around you: like happy children;

....love is pounding at the doors you hide behind: answer it;

....When loves comes clattering will I let it in: truthfully, **WHY**?

- love is made for *Two*: it has to be;

....Keep an *Open* heart: rambling;

..... and, you can find love: I know!

Take look around: open those *Eyes*; there will be love: promise;

....what I feel, I can't resolve now: *Strength*;

.....it will find a way back to your life: believe;

....Love has a plan, it was always there; you need time to see it surround you!

Why is love always stronger ... without you?

Tell me Why?

of Loving YOU:

Looking for _W_hat _is real, yet_

... my dreams are more than a memory to me.

...looking for what is _R_eal;

trying to remember the good .... and, the bad;

the _F_alling for you;

you becoming my world;

..... that dream made me _G_lad.

From this _P_oint of view;

..... my dreams are more real, the true deal;

...dreaming of what I have found;

....has _B_ecome more real.

Looking inside my _M_emories ..... I see so

much of what I know;

Your love .... made all my dreams _C_ome true,

...for this;

- I will always _remember_ you!

Look inside *Me*...

    ....and you will find dreamscapes filled with peace of mind;

In spite of what *Others* say;

I will find,

..... a way to love you even more.

Dreams of love have turned from fear;

  - I no long shed *Tears*;

and as I dream of love;

...... they are only of you *Dear*.

Looking for what was real;

  ..... I look inside my dreams for *Clarity*;

  ..... what I have found, we already know;

....some *Peace* of mind - in spite of what every-one said;

I have found the way......

... of Loving you More!

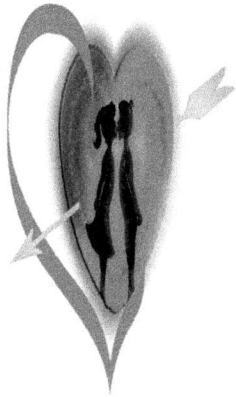

A desire to know HER:

As I travel through My memories;

...I reflect upon You.

Yes, *SHE* is beautiful;

- SHE has become *MY* religious experience;

......SHE is the beautiful character, filling volumes of *MY* books;

..SHE becomes the words;

.....and *HER* worth to ME is endless;

......being the purity of *MY* life are because of and, filled by HER;

......that are *Splattered* in ink across *MY* page.

SHE is the place I want to visit;

.....SHE is the beginning of MY journey;

.....a road trip I hope to be always perusing;

....*SHE* is MY first class flight;

* SHE is *MY* destination *

.....a locale where...... the sun burns the sand under *OUR* feet;

....yet the burning glow warms OUR hearts as *WE* gaze at OUR sanctuary;

...under the frond's of a swaying hammock'ed palm;

.....the Sun's glows turns from brilliant blues, to hazy *Sienna*;

....stars emerge to reunite with the *Moon* as they finally co-mingle;

...this day has become OUR lives' ...... mode de vie.

The morning *Sun* doesn't even change....

....all these days from co-mingling.

SHE is MY *Dream:*

....and knows how to make ME think of *HER*;

......In the early *Twilight* and, misty morning;

.......SHE has become *MY* endless *Fantasy*,

-- because, *SHE* knows ME.......!

.....There have been others but,

- - none, that know ME like this;

....It's just not being able to finish *MY* sentences,

...It is being the *Reason* for the

Sentence to begin with.

Love me Forever:

_...don't $\mathcal{M}$istake my interest as
passing $\mathcal{I}$nfatuation._

You gave me your hand;

....you never ask why I promise, all of my $\mathcal{W}$orld;

- there were never a question that WE would
live emphatically like $\mathcal{V}$ivaldi;

....in concert 'til we die; or

.... would _WE_ live in a relationship that was
deaf as $\mathcal{B}$eethoven....

-who became a $\mathcal{C}$omposer that could only hear
God's notes after he could $\mathcal{N}$o longer hear
$\mathcal{M}$ankind's music.

~ during our conclusion and when our backs were to
the $\mathcal{W}$all...

.... others separated us, pushed WE apart;

- they say all things will change, MY love for you
has always stayed the same...

- while _WE_ broke up, there were breaking
hearts;

... and $\mathcal{I}$mpeached souls;

- everyone was guilty;

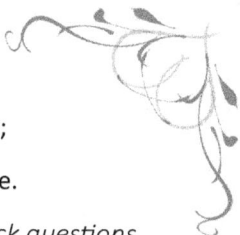

- everyone one was to *Blame*;

.....*And* no one was to blame.

~ all ways back to WE, brought back questions
WHY and then, HOW to get back to the start ~

- no one dies from a *Broken* heart yet...*no*
one is the same.

- we are the *Status*;

- we were the *Quo*!

- we made *Bad* .... good;

- like the *Worm* in the *Core*;

....another life is maintained ....from our
Sustain.

~ I don't ever remember laughing 'til **WE** *cried...*
together;

- maybe that was the *Pledge* unto death;

- that became a knife that was embedded in
OUR hearts.

Oh my lost love;

- tell *Me* no lies...

- ask me no *Questions* about why...

- send me no pleas and deals...

- you know you *Plundered* MY heart's love...
like a thief that steals...

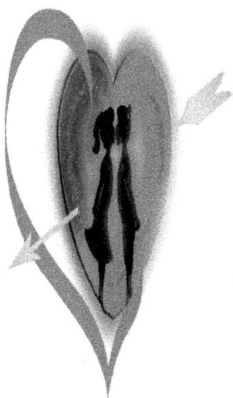

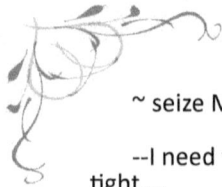

~ seize MY heart in your dreams *Tonight*....

--I need you to snatch my heart and clutch it tight....

....oh my *Love* ~

I LOVE YOU evermore....

hide and seek Love:

...... where I'm I going to hide from *Love*;

....I don't know but,

...... I know what it is like in *Purgatory*.

Love from *Yesterday*....

..... promises and *Ardent* words of hope;

...... hanging from a shadowy thread;

...... that sees our lives together;

..... all gather in a place where love from yesterday *Lingers*.....

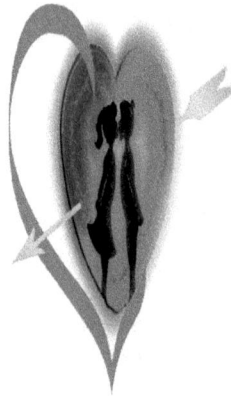

Love's Purgatory....

....you have beguiled my mind;

..... I can't squander more time on thinking about vacant love;

.....so, I go to my place where I search for answers;

... my *Dreams* of you!

- Though I *Never* recognize the insomnolence answers - they always come to light in my dreams;

....I wonder misty *Masquerading* heartbeat paths asking for strength;

..... *Searching* for the truth of lost love;

'Cause I know what it is.....

....to evermore drift a lonely emptiness of *Heartbreak*.

Here I go....

.....to ascertain what I already lived;

......finding the only answer I've ever perused from deep into my heart;

.....like a *Mirage* born to walk bewildered seeking a lifetime of answers.

* * * * *

My *Mind* is wrought-filled!

..... an' I've made up enough excuses;

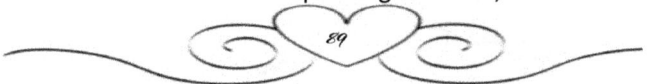

.... there are no more *Questions* asking why;

.... now, it is *Time* to move on;

...... it is time to do and not die.

I don't need an irrational redemption;

..... I am wanting answers;

... to *Questions* on *LOVE's* self-centered purgatory!

~ *I feel like....*

...... I have to search till the end of times;

.....'*Cause* you know what it means not to give up
one a love that is just beyond reach; so

......I am *Big-eyed* roaming the desolate sea of
dreamy *Nights*!

An' I've decide in my mind....

..... I am not searching in places with no answers;

...... *Not* one more time.

so, I go *Again*.....

....traveling the only *Path* that makes me whole;

...like Halley's comet stretching across the
Universe;

....waiting to find a final destination for my answers;

..... *Clearly* I am only to return again and again;

.... time without *End*.

'Cause I know what it answers....

..... I ain't searchin' no more;

....searching for the meaning of *Love*....

For Me:

...it is

.....being

...... *Happy* to be detached!

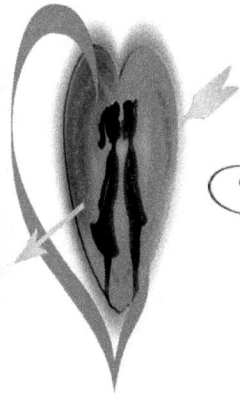

keep Me close:

.....I need to Know,

if YOU WILL take my breath and

never let me go...!

- No matter what, no matter when....

I would do it all over again....

Tell me I'm still the ONE!

'*Cause* you know I want nothing else;

Then to have you to myself;

a jealous and zealous beast;

you can rely.

I may be *Selfish* AND,

 .... I caused your pain;

  ..... instead of finding weakness;

   ..... I'll be your search of worthiness.

*****

Your love is all I ever desired,

if you still feel it....

..... NOW it's all I want to do is *Hear* it.....

- I will be there, every day;

- and in loving moments, as I bite my lip;

- you'll know this.....

- is something beyond *Bliss*.....

   And,

 - if you choose to stay.....give me a reason to believe;

 - you'll be there in the *Morning*;

- it doesn't matter *How* the story ends;

- as long you are by my *Side*.

*****

if our love stays young ... it can't grow old;

.... it's *Love* !

.... that's all I want to hear you say;

.... I *Will* always feel this way.

I'll want to make it feel...

like the First time;

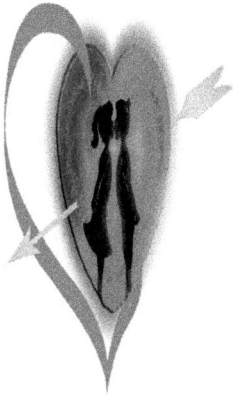

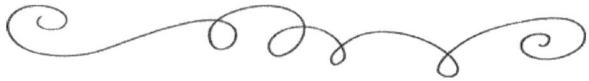

The World was Your oyster:

It was as if the *World* just

stopped ....

- I dressed in finery and gold;

.... and I made my *Own* rules;

....my world was all about conquering with just a smile; one day at a time;

.....one of carnal frenzy filled with shadowed approach to another level of society;

....you're not that child of God no mo;

....you aren't just accountable for you and you alone;

....it is about all the others;

....it IS not just you, by *Yourself*!

- I harrow for the days of old;

...when there was just your beauty by my side;

... reliving these dreams in the mist;

..... I *Can't* resist.

* * * * * *

~ *From You*....

....freedom is a kiss;

.... that led me to remember the days when it was just you and I;

- in *Unison*.

....a relationship that I wish I had today ... more each and every DAY.

- there is something out there;

...every second of our *Nights*;

..... I lived another life;

... in a society filled by pressure and stress;

- my relief valve is you and us;

...being helped by you saying that:

Everything that is you, is ME... !

...You being the mortal that you have turned into agrees with my consciousness;

... happiness is my outcome.

* * * * * * *

- Funny how your feet never touch the earth as your angelic Essence wafts over the flora that makes up our bedroom's carpet...

- In a life brimming of *Prince's*;

...all have to hide their faces because your *Beauty* is so overwhelming, they can't bear to agree, that there isn't another who can command US all with just a glance.

- every moment I'm awake;

.....the further I'm taken from my *Belle*;

....these dreams go on when my mind is open full of happiness as my eyes are closed;

....now, I can only live in these dreams, that continue to hide away my real feelings when it's bright outside.....!

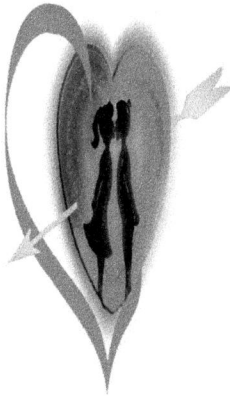

LOVE's hope:

~ has there be a time where we

can fall out of Love ~

..... in HOPE's inexhaustible *Flame*, MY spirit is burning bright - in the ember's glow - that was once US;

~ my mind's eye is chasing a heartfelt moment ~

..... like a fluttering moth in the wind;

...... striving to reach a flame;

.... only to find this flame once *Slayed*.

- - Within the embers of OUR flame.....a *Glow*;

~ *Bounced* between the once barren walls of MY tortured mind ~

......as it weaves a spidery cloak, like a *Surreal* dream;

..... it then became the merest, mournful breeze;

.... reminiscent of a misty winter's stream;

.....it's passing, like the *Ebb* of tides, the cloak glimmered;

.....causing the glow to diminish yet, *Not* falter!

~ as *Months* and *Years* pass ~

- the *Flicker* of our flame only quivered;

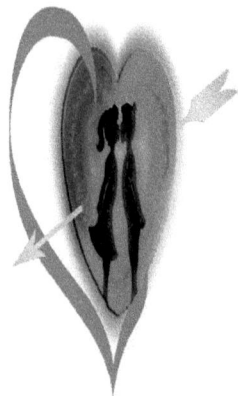

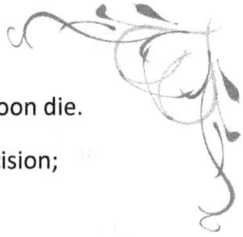

....like it was choosing whether to soon die.

..... unable, I had stop to make a decision;

- at last my aim was *Straight*;

..... my hand plunged into my chest;

.....*Snatching* out my beating heart;

.... to assuredly jettison this dying ruthless hope.

~ *Surviving* - a lingering sound struggled

to *Emerge* ~

....arising from abruptly scant beats;

....a single voice - from my *Conspicuous* heart;

- was clear above the din,

- that fills an empty room - that was once my heart's purgatory.

....a single scant sound that tells of my will to sustain...

..... OUR eager voices had become the single ardent strand of tapestry where *Two* hearts to once more spin delicate knots that tie OUR SOUL's as one.

- OUR *LOVE* has become the forlorn strand of silk;

...... that was once abandoned NOW, creates a crowning *Bond*;

.....our life's tapestry started our habitual LOVE;

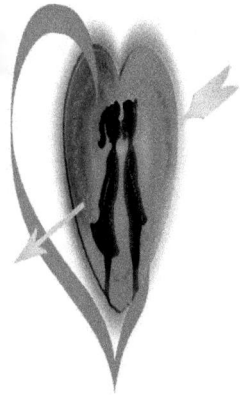

...... *Our* thoughts are the hands that weave time and lives together as one;

..... an enduring LOVE is the single *Pulse* that was suppressed within our once vacant flicker;

..... it was purgatory's fire - within this flame - that burns all we can LOVE.

~ Is this the *end* or are we just *beginning* ~

**** Here is to our newly united****

.....*our cups overflowing without Yesterday's Sorrowful remorse - are raised to a jovial toast - made to yet again to bless a union of Matched Soul's.*

WE ARE HAPPY FOR THEM!

Is it Enough:

.... It's NOT about the daily toil.

When we say some necessities to each other but, is it *Enough*???

I need .... a furious love affair with YOU ... that fills my nights with dreams that are as *Vibrant* as YOU made love making for me when we're first married.

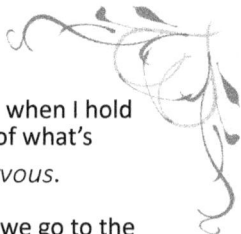

* I want ... My hands to sweat when I hold your hand because ... the anticipation of what's going to happen next makes me *Nervous*.

** I want ... to feel that when we go to the ocean to watch the sunset; it feels commonplace and deliciously repetitious.

*** I want ... people to see us as a couple and say; look at them.... *They* must have just got married.... *(they are still so in love)*

** the most *Important* thing is **

...when you look at me ....

* I want ... to see in your eyes .... a *Love*-struck wife...

** all I ever wanted ..... is to feel your loving thoughts...

-- like when big 10 inch plays on the radio;

...and I see that devilish-brat face you made!

****

How did we get along?

* Did we have that once in a lifetime *Spark*?

... did you need to let me know it was there;

-falling into each other's arms every night;

- did we lose ourselves every night;

....was all-night cuddling a set rule to our sleeping pattern.

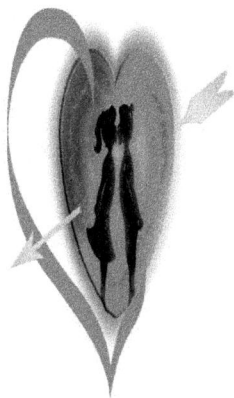

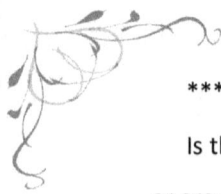

*** Is it *Enough*? ***

Is this what we have left being a couple?

...or are we living through *Dreams* of the past?

* Is this what love really is for US now?

** Yelling hugs through dreams hoping the other will hear?

*** Telling one another the other person's idea of bliss?

**** And dreaming up scenarios where we could be happy someday?

-- it is as though we starve OUR love for someday and feed lustful wishes of SOMETIME through *Dreams*....

... Is it enough?

- I wish we'd consummate;

- those lazy nights together endlessly teasing of you ;

... let me heal you like no one else can;

And,

I'll kiss away your fears and worries.

...I wonder where is the *Bliss*?

- why can't I be content for - "maybe soon" ?

-- because my mind has never let you be someone else's *Wife*!

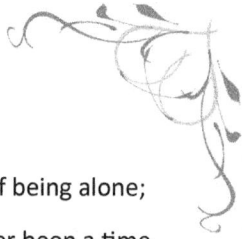

.... *Though;*

- I have always had a feeling of being alone;

.... although there has never been a time where I thought to *Myself* - this isn't all there should be!!!

.....why does it have to be a *Struggle*?

- to love one another when;

- it is supposed to be....you got married because you could not see yourself with another person!

-- this is not enough!

-- it is not *Enough*!

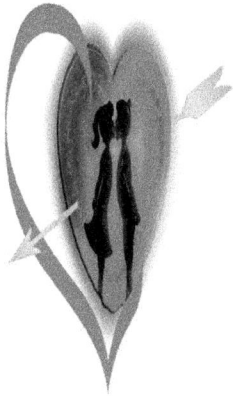

There is nothin' that lets you Forget like Love:

before we say adieu....

...*Give* me a little time;

And in my arms you might find;

a love like the ONE you knew;

....when *Our* lives were just us two.

When we said goodbye, I sadly watched you walk away....

....all of the plans we made;

became so many tears rolling down.

...In the shadows of my waking dreams all alone;

I watched as you get along.

I should have grabbed you and said:

- take one more chance on *Me*...

but, done is done.

and, that was a past romance...

I thought......!

What makes someone forget about love *Lost* ....

...It was the next *Love* to turn around your frown.

....It's over now, I thought for such long a time;

You've cried enough - I said to myself, it will be fine ... give it time.

....Someday, Somewhere and Someone new ... in my arms ...

- I'll find the ONE that lets me forget this pain;

but, NOTHING made me *Forget* about our love;

Then....

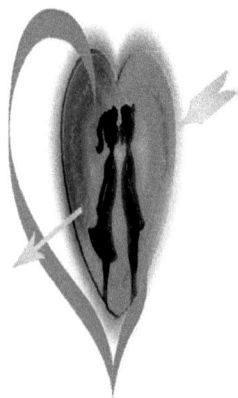

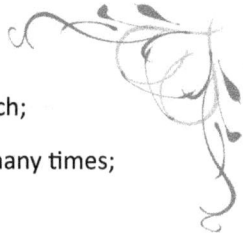

- a human heart, can only take so much;

- I halted to pick the pieces, too many times;

.... I thought to start again;

- New people with the hope of *New* love ....
over and over I tried;

..... they were lies.

My *Mind* said;

... let me strike a bonfire - to the past so my
anguish can dance inside those flames .....

for so long, even the *Devil* said "*that's bad ass*".

Once you feel a love that is real....

You just can't recall the 'cause....

...nothing lets you forget about, first *Love*.

- *It's* over now, my heart cried enough....but,

give me a little more time;

- and, someone new in arms you'll find;

.... maybe one more time.

*Nothing makes you forget about lost love like
renewed love!*

I know it's hard to reach...

- for someone that you knew so long ago;

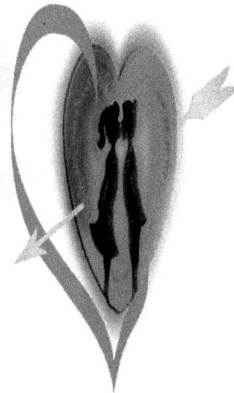

.... close your eyes;

Trust your heart;

And,

let love go through a new *Test*....

"*It's over*"; you've cried enough - is enough;

Is it time to *Start* anew?

- *this could be the best!*

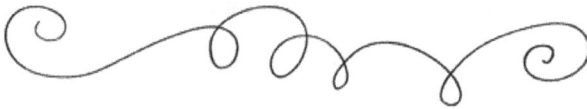

Maybe I'm Sadly hallow about my Thirst:

I feel awkward wanting someone....!

.....now I'm gazing at your picture;

asking myself how could I stop thinking of you?

.....As if I could surrender my *Strength*.

...... I never dared give so much of myself .... to anyone before;

.....my *Mancard* was in crisis....

- You have seen the awkward bits of myself ... like nobody has before.

YOU know *Me* and now
...my *Thirst*:

.....it is a more a comfortable feeling;

.....just being me, nakedly barefoot;

.....the first thing you see in the morning;

.....you made me feel *Handsome*;

....just being the guy that you stood by;

- made me proud every day -- *that you choose me*!

.....I didn't always feel that way then yet, I do now!

To Us:

- - When somebody just *Loves* you;

......and when you can make somebody happy ..... just being in their presence;

I suddenly feel like the most

important person.

Does a thirst ever stop -- the *Wanting* you?

.....when you just up and left;

....everything went crazy ..... with my wanting you;

- the *Kisses* - your passion - all melting together;

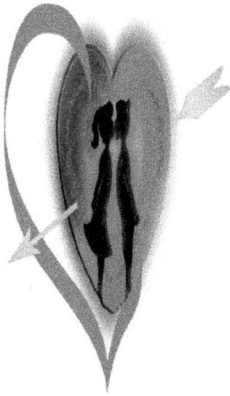

.....being held together by you just by you constantly being by my side;

....you were there for the *Strange* and the struggle.

....Immature love says: "I love you because I need *You*."

....*Mature* love says "I need *You* because I *Love* you."

And, now I'm looking at you....

....my heart is *Asking* if I still need you;

.....as if I could stop longing for you;

....as if I could give up the thing that makes me strong?

To You:

...... I never dared give to another as much;

...I have never separated from you completely;

I still belong to You .... Always.

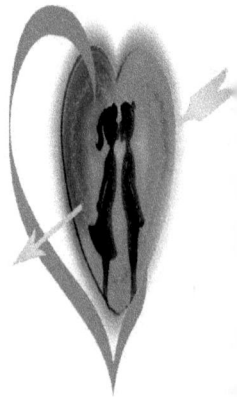

My love is there for You:

...am $\mathcal{I}$ ready for $\mathcal{L}$ ove?

A $\mathcal{H}$ eart needs love;

...to be in and to need - $\mathcal{L}$ ove.

But is it love that your heart needs?

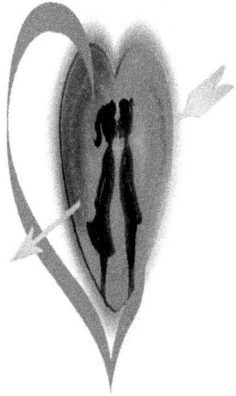

...an $\mathcal{E}$ mpty heart; without love for another, feels like meandering in an empty container the size of a auditorium.

..... It is like that empty room, was filled with memories like a Witches' wispy spell fills a seemingly empty cauldron with a $\mathcal{F}$ aint poof;

.......empty as a stadium the day after a big game - nothing left but the liter;

....What would this hallow be without love - to fill the spaces emptied from a lifelong $\mathcal{T}$ ryst;

....without you, by my side I am empty; without you, I can't tell who I should be;

.......Tell me! If I knew, I would tell you!

Tell $\mathcal{M}$ e;

- what is my life without your love?

- walking this road without end;

- perplexed by how my life would proceed;

-where it could lead;

- if you are nearby;

.....it will be one that is full!

To capture your love is my
Greatest prize of all.

- My heart hunts like an animal: searching;

   - not unlike a cheetah running down it's prey: capture;

   - our hearts were brought *Together* like a pen is to an empty sheet of paper: fulfilled;

   - I know what I can do ... stay and tell you why: hope;

....like Curtis Lowe - that was *Drawn* to a bottle of wine and a guitar melody;

        .....my life has become filled by confessing these stories of love ... for you!

   - The heart has the final Say -

   .....our life together has brought Feelings of
   Joy to this once caressed Soul.

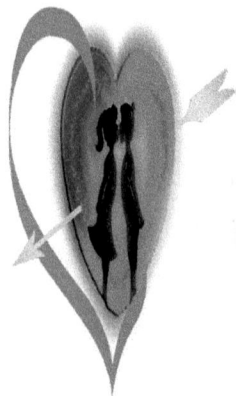

a Persistent LOVE:

a lost LOVE's battlefield...

....after you say I LOVE you - again!!! ... what more can be said?

....LOVE scars us all.

... lost of LOVE *Marks* and *Wounds* our souls for all *Eternity*;

...wounds to the heart are battlefield tested and eventually lived past;

- living through and *Past* passion's triage;

...I have now found why people say; "what doesn't kill you makes you stronger."

.....It is not only befitting, it is an *Everlasting* one.

......if you are lucky enough to *Fall* in LOVE with equal measure, there are risks for letting someone in to share your deepest thoughts, hope's and glories;

....it empowers your life's wisdom when you love with your whole heart and share in the bliss of LOVE's torture.

...*Risks* of LOVE....

~ Any heart not tough enough to withstand love's unending urgent *Demands*, has undoubtedly experienced my plight ~

.....every heart risks liabilities to experience LOVE's misery and glory

....with LOVE comes strife;

...it is as predictable as gray clouds full of rain;

.....at *Some* point, it will pour!

Lovelorn minds tell their souls;

...like a rebel without a *Cause*;
...hurt feelings are just part of life's initiation.

* * * * * *

I know a thing or two

about Love's pain.

....I have been well-versed at this from missing my paired heart;

..... that ache is a *Lifelong* enduring sentence.

....I have deflected pain's harm through my sarcasm and secretive jokes that always tell a story of *Woe*...

.....LOVE is like a flame, it can burn you when everything is *Hot* and, again when it is not.

is LOVE a Fool's game....

....Some fools *Think*....life's commitment to the heart is of happiness, blissfulness and is emblematic with togetherness;

....Some fools fool themselves, they can't fool me;

.... I know what isn't in a grasp of love: is and what was my *Lie*;

....I know and hope there is more;

.....*Someone* different ... *Somewhere* different;

....there has to be a spirit that matches my will to find it.

~ *a thirsty passion ..... Cannot just be a lie made to make you dream of absent LOVE;*

~ LOVE hurts the one that seeks out its rewards without paying the cost of first a *Broken* heart. ~

******

Loving *Patience*.....

...is not sitting and waiting, it is foreseeing;

....it is looking for disappointment and *Finding* joy;

- - that is my present-day *Quest*;

it is like....

.... searching a condo lined *Beachfront*;

- only being able to see the sand and waves;

- - washing onshore with the flowing ebb of *Renewed* hope;

- - - a place of peace and everlasting joy, is followed by changing awakenings....

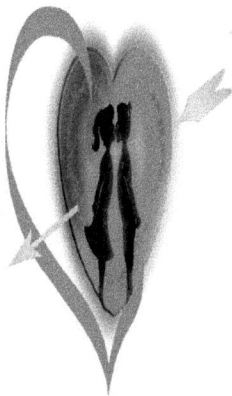

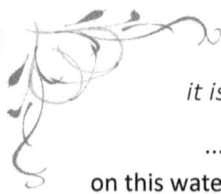

it is.... Love

... where all see the daydreams of a child;
on this water's edge... and *Love* is to see the world
through their eyes; it is so expansive, beautifully
bright and full of renewed hope;

- It is: looking past the *Thorns* to see
only the *Rose* because; without the thorns you
wouldn't handle this delicate flower so gently;

- It is: looking at the din of a Night's *Romance*
and only being able to see days filled with memories
of youthful LOVE.

Needing Love ... there is always the need for
patience - for LOVE to flourish;

- It is: the moon needs time - so can soon
become full;

- It is: the heart never loses real LOVE;

- It is: we have lost many years yet, not
years filled with real LOVE.

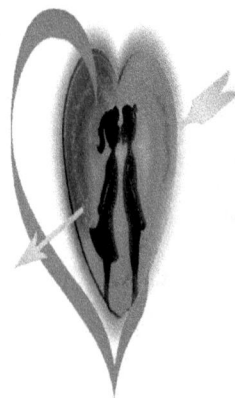

~ It stays locked inside our

hearts ready for whenever

you are strong enough

...to Find it again ~

**Remembering:**

_I found a picture of what it must be like just
before you go to sleep on your couch....
I am in Heaven!_

- Just thinking that this is you and you took
a minute to think about me to send me a little
tempting picture like this....;-)

That might not mean that much to you...
except to _Remind_ me that you remember me
enough - to send a note saying:

....that you are there waiting there for me!

*****

_Remembering and doing are
two different things..._

*****

* I remember a lot *

- a _Picture_ like this reminds me of what
we did have and could have had if I kept more focus
on the important things. YOU!

.....it could have been a relationship with a
spark that still sizzles, one that makes my mind spin
with _Pleasures_ - that await.

When you go out of your way to send me a
reminder about what I have waiting for me when I
get home - something I sometimes overlooked

I wish our relationship was still one high-
lighted by playful _Sexy_ notes - that you send me
- to remind me I have you waiting for me at home.

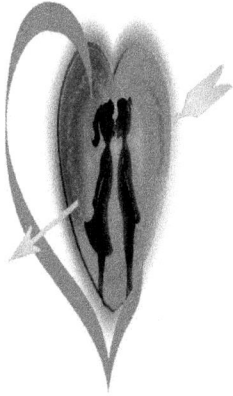

Maybe you're sneaking into my car, waiting for me to get out of work, was just overlooked by me as a silly prank .... I should have taken advantage of the *Devotion* that you exuded to make a spark in the relationship when you did something *Uncommon* and memorable.

Your day was probably filled with questions of why does he always have to be away so much?

......It was the life I choose; I always believed it is the career that chooses you; my Parents, Uncle and Grandfather followed the same path as I...

.....Now, my children have been caught up in the same *Zest* for the *Jazz* of this career.

... I know that there is a future for them because; they do take time away from work to commit to their other halves.

I know that if I had someone as beautiful as my daughters waiting for me at home, I would think twice about staying extra time at work.

Oh, I did have a Woman like that!

What was my problem?

...I am just a *Workaholic*!

I feel the commitment made to my job is all-encompassing and, all consuming.

That is my fault and advantage.

I want to do a good job at what I have become; now I realize that the job doesn't wait for you at home with a *Smile* and a loving touch.

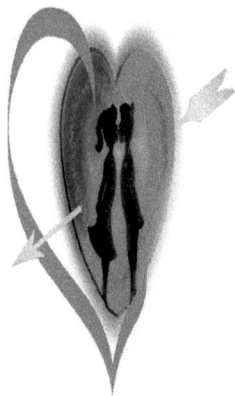

.....You were!

.....Now, I see that it could have been so different for us if I was dedicated more to us.

......You were *Young*, I was *Hungry*.

......I needed to excel at everything.
......*I now tell myself I should have tried excelling at making you my Wife.*

****

"We were *Young*" only goes so far anymore.
"We were too young to understand" is not good enough.
...What is it that makes for commitment ..... to another person?

.....It is remembering, even when things are hectic, to drop a note to remind them that you are *Thinking* about them.....all the time?

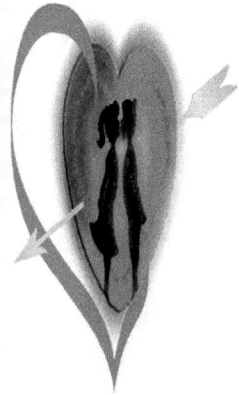

Love is gone and the words (w)right themselves;

.... they feed the paper with emptiness;

....one that was once _Clear_ is now dark with messages of an _Empty_ spirit.

- I don't know where love has gone but, it is not in my marrow anymore.

- I just want to be _Alone_ with this outpouring of thought and faceless words....

- It is a simple thing to hide behind words of love; it is something else living by those words....

....that is why being alone is easy;

.... If you want; you get;

... without thought of what others desire.

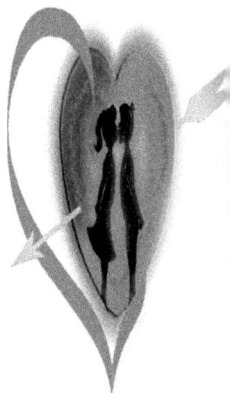

I'm leaving that love alone with my bereft affections;

......somehow I know it will depart on its own;

...being alone is the only part me that makes my resolution complete.

Alone with my thoughts;

.... I'm able to stealthily become someone that everybody expects me to be;

-- For now,

....I sit and stare at a page of my life that is becoming more and more disheveled stated;

....It is there because my number one is gone and all I can do is stare;

.....my baby is gone and I can't find another because, no one compares.

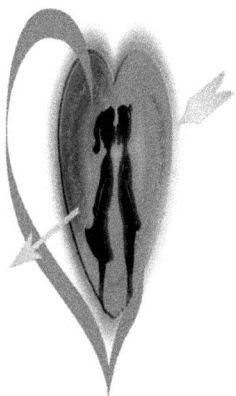

Chapter Three:

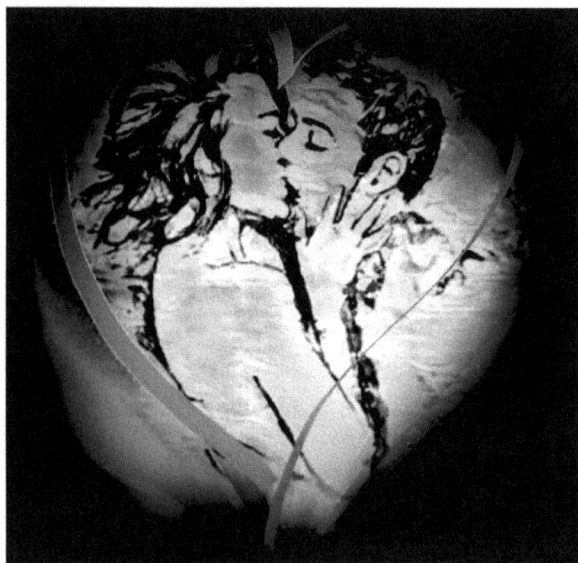

Dreaming...

I use to dream and wake:

just to see if you were

still next to me...

....I watched over you while you slept all night;

.... so peaceful; reassured me that what we had was right;

.....You might...

..... have been far off dreaming of *C*astles and princes at night.... but;

......my world revolves around my ONE *Q*ueen, you my dear!

....I could spend the rest of my life in this moment;

... that I will forever not fear;

...so many years have past;

.....my dreams are now just of you my *D*ear;

...staying lost in these dreams with you;

.... makes me feel like we are still near.

....I never want to miss a wide-eye

reality like this;

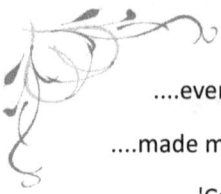

....every moment spent seeing you next to me;

....made me happier than any other heartfelt bliss;

....'Cause lovin' you is the *Sweetest* dream;

....that I could never resist;

.....even when I dream without you here;

......my heart still insists;

....there has got to be away;

..... to reconcile that won't be insidious.

I always wonder.....

... Would I rather be missing you in my dreams?

....my heart says don't bother;

...you will always have dreams of a FIRST LOVER.

I still miss you, like no other;

....my heart only wants to know if it is the same for any other lover;

.....there is someone up above who commands with a silent mutter;

....deep within OUR specter.

Dreams and all my senses:

....it all started kind of $\mathcal{W}$eird even for my dreams.

I was in a beautifully decorated bar; a restaurant bar. It was nearly night time; dusk.

The place is masculine in decor, steakhouse look with deep dark wooden walls with beautifully polished marble accents. I have never been in a place that looked exactly like this one did but, it was so memorable I had to add it, if just to help set up scene so you can understand the feel of the dream.

The bar was crowed, full of people then; you appeared out of nowhere. It was like ... what are you doing in $\mathcal{C}$hicago? What the hell was I doing in Chicago?

I didn't know what happened to the answer, my mind was lost. It was fixated on you. You look stunning ... with those fashionably sexy heels that made your rear so sexy.

I was in a $\mathcal{T}$rance!!!!

Then, I remembered and thought to myself what are you doing just standing here looking stupid. Why are you aren't you doing something? Say something at least, say something intelligent!!! ugggg!

...this is the $\mathcal{C}$onversation I am having with myself (in my head) ... as my own dream is unfolding.

I move closer, you smile. At the same time that I'm staring at you, I am slowly backing you against the wall.

I pull your arms over your head and pin your wrist to the wooden wall.

I stand there amazed at the way you look tonight. In my head I'm going through all these scenarios of what I should do.

I am thinking to myself in my dream .... How, is this possible?

You are just as beautiful as when we separated over 30 years ago. I can't help myself but to stare deeply into your eyes.

Your *Face* is now beaming because ... *in this dream* ... you can read my thoughts .

...I am thinking and you React simultaneously.

It is so hot ....that you know what I am going to do and; you are beaming with that mischievous *brat* smile because you actually like what I am thinking about doing to you.

It is so hot; being able to *Communicate* my thoughts without stumbling over words.

I am getting so turned on in my dream that, I'm thinking to myself, does she know how sexy this is for me .... that; she is reading my mind and she actually likes whatever I am thinking?

.... I am going through this in my head ... in my dream.

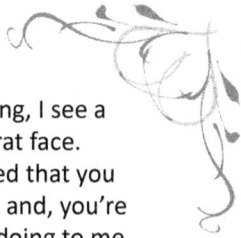

Because you know what I'm thinking, I see a smirk build on that ever-so beautiful brat face.

Now, you know that... I just realized that you know ... what I'm thinking in my dream and, you're smiling because you can see what it is doing to me by the look on my face. It becomes contagious, as we trade smirks.

I am there continuously - for 3 or 4 maybe 5 minutes - I lose track of time; looking at you looking at me.

As we are doing this and you are reading my thoughts (in this dream)
...all the sudden we change locales.

We appear at this place where I've been before..... It is in Key West.

It is in a hotel and we have a private suite that I have to describe to you it is so beautiful.

Today is bright and the room is filled with a light that just can't be described because of the amount of setting sunlight is bursting in our room.

This room is a giant suite on the top floor of this hotel. It is at the very end of Duval Street ... which is the farthest point you can go to the south west on *Key West* .... and it is famous for sunset watching.

The room is large but the main point is that we get transferred from the place that we were just at in Chicago and sent ... my dream to this room .... in the shower. It is not just any ordinary shower.... this has towering river stone laid walls and is enclosed by 9 foot glass walls.

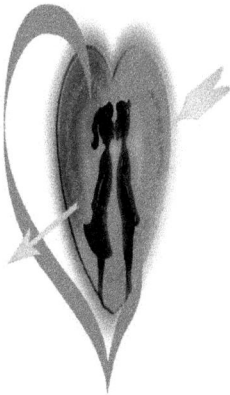

It is a beautiful shower steamy and hot and you're there and.... I am just amazed at how beautiful you look with the steam surrounding you.

The beads of perspiration that are traversing your naked body.... going across your so tight sexy abdomen and ... your butt is *so hot*. Your face is so beautiful even with the shower running; your makeup is perfect, your hair is still perfect.

I'm amazed at how this is happening and again you are smiling at me because, you can still read my thoughts.

It is so...so...Soooooo hot that you know what I am thinking.

Again I am in a trance staring at you. This whole Scenario leads me to think ... about the beauty of this situation.

I just know that .... you know ....what I'm thinking and it's even more intimate that we can communicate without talking. You know what I'm thinking and.... you know that I am absolutely so in love with you right now. We are so close and so passionately groping each other!

The scene seems unreal to me and I'm thinking that in my dream and then of course you know what I'm thinking and you say be quiet! You are thinking this out too much! Let's just be together and not think about what tomorrow or what the next 2 hours is going to hold for us. Let's just be together and enjoy the moment.

In my mind I am admitting to myself ... I am in love .... And, you can feel it too.

I'm looking around and this steam has envelope this entire 10 foot by 10 foot shower. The walls that made out of the river rock with green wood with tan highlights and are simmering with all the humidity that is pouring out from the shower. It makes for elegant scenery... *Surrounding* us ....with steam that you can just barely see through across the shower because the damn shower so large.

This steam also makes you glisten just... shine incredibly sexy-hot, did I mention incredibly hot... I am so turned on by how beautiful you look it is like somebody oiled you down with *Steam*.

I am so turned on in my dream and you start smiling even more because you know *Exactly* what I am thinking without me having to say a word and it makes you smile and then you say I am as happy as you because I know right now that *You* love me and you can tell that I think you're the most beautiful thing I've ever seen before in my life.

I don't have to say a word you just tell me that I know exactly what I'm thinking and then you start telling me exactly what is in my head and I can't believe it. This is the perfect dream because I don't have to fumble with my thoughts and jumbled the words. Words always get in the way... and now I don't have to think about how my words going to make you react before I say them.

You can't Imagine how turned on I am by not having to fumble through a vocabulary and speak in a way that is passionate and says what I truly mean.

I could just feel what I feel and you like ... no; you Love what I am thinking.

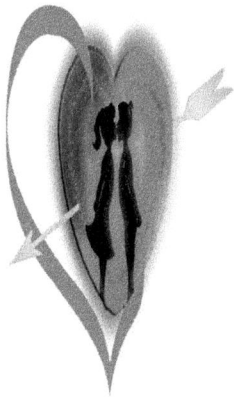

This is an incredibly sexy dream for me just knowing that you like everything I'm thinking about and of course it's about sex but it isn't about having sex; it is about the most intimate part of sex. Being *Sensual* and knowing exactly what somebody else likes and agreeing with it and urging more of the same thoughts.

Miss you:

I *Miss* you to a *Point* of nil;

...void, yet invariably in my *Dreams* I am by your side;

... I'm listening but there's never sound, yet my dream is understood by us both;

... again falling short of rage, and my heart pulse is made stable with you by my side;

.... a frenzied mania ready to erupt, and again thoughts and dreams keep me harmonized;

....there's something out there - I can't see it now;

.....I thought I would be there by now, decade later I still *Wonder*;

.....hopelessness....won't lead me towards your heart;

....It must be that empathy, trying to interpret this uprooted life;
  -- this is supposed to be the point of dreams!

There's a certain kind of emptiness that has satiated my *Life*;
    ....what is life supposed to be - if it isn't deluge with thoughts of you?
       .... tryin' to recover.
    ....Take me to a place in my life ... that feels replete with a centuries-old bloodline;
      .....I don't know where you might have been;
      .... I'm with you now- if only in a dream.

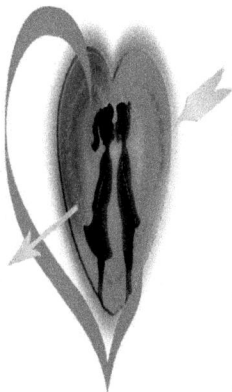

Missing you...
    ....means missing your eyes;
    .... the way they revel in saucy glee;
     ....when I see you;
       ....those eyes! ... your contemptuous smirk that shrouds my sanity;
     ....it all brings me to a place of resolute order;
      .....worthy and unimpaired with harmony and balance.

It is *Primal*...
    ....to be needed by the one that begets love's thirst;
      .....it drives one to suspect singularity.

- - that was my dream last night...."in my life"
    ....missing YOU has brought my mind to wander at night about that bratty spirit...

....one that has been there when we were new to love and; then again through life's changes.

******

......it was a bright day like any other seen in the fall.
- why was it important to mention it was fall because,

-- we saw all the annoying *X*mas decorations already up in the stores.
-- not that Xmas is annoying, it is annoying because they go up sometime before the Halloween mask even come down.
- when you saw this and said - with that face that could only be described as bratty;
-- "well that is capitalism for you".

-Reminding me it is all about business and not being able to have one holiday at a time. We are always out shopping, again!
-- it is what we do!

Not just shopping at the usual local market;

... it was this elaborate place with *F*lowing curtains that were so tall - endless actually;
... as we are walked through these flowing velvety partitions - to the next passageway to another shop;
-- We stop; you promise all this shopping will be worth it for me...
...I know it will....
in this fantasy, I wanna reiterate that I expect my usual payment for going shopping all day with you...
Garvin style!!!

.... shopping with you use to be a drudgery but,
....now, that you know it made me feel pathetic you figured out a way for me to continue on for hours.

...*Sex!* of course you made it all about sex.

-- You know what it means for me to be with you;
--- I love how you have stretched out our outing;
-- to make this more about how you can be as bratty as possible;
-- and keep me at the edge of my patients and excited about the whole afternoon - at the same time!

....This is why you will always my *Bratty* girl.
....You know you can get away with pushing my buttons and;

.... I am still here to see how you are going to push the next one.

...this story continues!

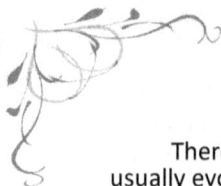

Saint in Lace:

There is always a *Story* behind the story; usually evoked by me by saying something off the *Wall*.....

.....because I am absolutely in love with the way you look. I have to deflect my headstrong innuendos to play down being so enthralled with the way you appear to me.

.....this *Dream* opens innocently enough;

That tells me you are my Saint in Lace....

Your dressing in *Lace* only goes to enhance my lusty thoughts of why I am having this dream. Your curves and all those *Beautiful* spots that I adore on you ... I know are just under the sheer lace; that *Enhance* your curves, as the material seems as whimsical as it is free spirited - in as much as your entire attire waifs in the slightest of breezes.

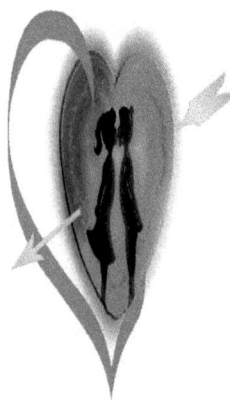

As usual I am thinking how is it possible that I have such a *Beautiful* woman waiting for me - to get *Home* and ...... loves to dress in ways that make you more *Enticing* to me ;

- I can do anything but just lean back and stare at you;

- I am bemused by watching you do nothing at all;

- I can't do anything but Stare.

- - I feel like a total dope.

~ You glide about the room casually proceeding like you don't have a care yet have an expression on your face that says you are lost in a daydream.

I can't believe I am here with you and seemingly without you knowing - maybe this is why you're doing this; maybe you don't know.

...I a so amazed at your *Beauty* that I don't say or make a sound;

....I am just they're hiding in plain site - just being there with you is justification enough for me to absolve that I might be considered a stalker for doing this....

.... It is a little weird; like I have melted into the paneled walls - I finally realize that is why you can't see me - camouflaged like this heightens my feeling that this is wrong. I don't bother asking myself why anymore, I just watch this proceed without a word.

.... You have a *Questioning* look and are trying to decide why you don't feel alone;

... you think I don't notice what you're doing;

- there's nothing further from the truth, I'm watching *Every* movement;

..... the *Slightest* change in your expression or wave of your hand; leads me to dream of endless possibilities to what will be next.

*****

...if this was not a *Dream* I would be saying to you every day:

....I wish you would *Stay*;

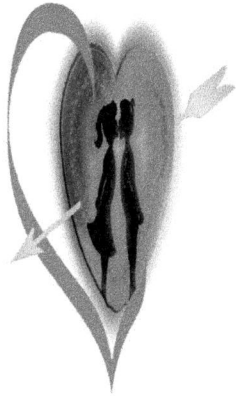

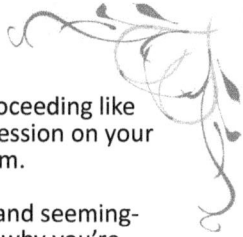

..... Stay with me another day, stay;

.... Stay with *Me* just stay!

...... I wanna *Hear* you say: I'll be there today, I'll stay!

......Cause I'd give anything to hear you *Say*:

.... We will *Stay* here together.

~ There has been times - with *Tears* on my pillow - from dreaming that you didn't stay;

....I have cried rivers 'cause your *Love* is wicked: when it is not mine;

....missing all the kisses is *Heartless* 'cause you don't know it is as wondrous as your beauty is excessive;

.......I await for you and,

.....Can't sleep *Because* you are always in my *Dreams*:

~ there is *Pain* in my heart when you haven't been in my dreams!

Once I was thought of as an Animal:

.....my dreams have $\mathcal{P}$*roven this animal has to sway from it is true feelings to seek it is way to the truth...*

$\mathcal{E}$nvisioning my dreams reminiscent of instances when life was guided by my passionate indication;

...today these dreams go on even when I close my $\mathcal{E}$yes;

- my $\mathcal{B}$eastly life irrevocably started when my dreams made me realize this animal is two personalities in one creature.

- my $\mathcal{D}$reams gave this creature the ability to be something more than what people saw in the $\mathcal{L}$ight.

- as last night's exodus from my feral side started it should have warned me what my dreams could $\mathcal{M}$ean.

.....at night I live another $\mathcal{L}$ife;

- one that has me feeling mortal.

......It started as I was peering into a sea of darkness;

....on the edge of where shadows have no end, I shield a candle in my grasp to lighten this egress through this seemingly unending passage.

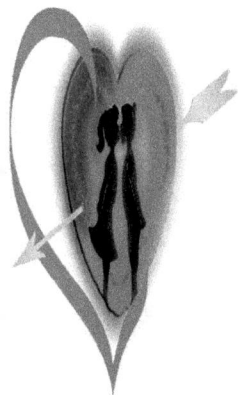

- my eyes strain and sharpen to see an uncertain figure ahead;

   - I struggle to see lucidly, I need to wait till it comes closer;

   - there is something out there; I can't resist but letting my mind wonder;

         - is it another animal or human?

  - I need to divert the agony in my mind;
.....stemming from previous encounters with beings in this darkening woodland;

    - *Where* I stand, my head swivels around;

   - moving in the trees, my eyesight is clumsily focusing;

    - as gentile as a butterfly; YOU move without a sound.

    - my eyes validate my heart's *Glee*, now elevated to give a palpable murmur;

    - as my animal eyes focus upon you;

   - I peer into YOUR eyes as they become my *Shangri-La.*

        ...... I can't look away without sabotaging my waking psyche!

      ....these dreams go on when my *Eyes*

         ...are wide shut:

  - *in these dreams,* this beast's primitive *Words* - that have no form - falling from my lips without direction or intent;

- I find the sweetest unwritten *Song* -is the one of the silence - while you are in my grasp; I am at peace!

.....every moment I'm in this dream, the more robust this beast's indentured *Heart* clings to *You*.

But all I remember;

....are the fleeting dreams in a murky morning glare, *Contorting* into a cognizant awake;

- an enigmatic *Dungeon* had kept this creature from breaking through to this cognizance;

....with your help, without a cut;

- this beast can cross through a crystalline stained glass-like cage;

- only to *Realize*, my dreams can be more important than living heartlessly in any waking hour;

..... I continually search for the time until I am able to live in this *Dreamscape* again;

- where this animal becomes a human with you as my emancipator.

.......*Where* this beast longs for the past and craves for the times with you by my side.

.....*Dreaming*:

- she brightens every lonely night, unendingly none are evermore the same;

- so lift up your heart; my voice says to my primitive brain....

- led by my thoughts ... away goes my heart again;

- *Leave*, leave now; the future has yet past us by!

- *go and seek out the one who makes you human!*

I know I'm a fool for you but, my carnal focus is *Apparent*;

.....once, not that long ago, a word, a touch; from you, and my world was complete. No matter the cost, I'll atone for a slight of your charms.

....."my docile *Animal*, dreamily gaze into your window towards an era with your charmed one. You've changed, you're not so far away from human"...

- - Become the man your *Heart* can deliver.

Dreams of you today were

once my reality:

-- *loving another has never been on my timetable.....like you were!*

- - *my dreams;*

....you have always been my *Fantasy*...

- they don't appear on command;

.....there always seems to be a plan in them;

- they don't have dockets...I try to meet;

- they don't come indivisibly with subtext to explain the answers I seek.

- they cohabit things in reciprocally ... until you look at them *Sequestered*;

- my dreams always have obstacles for me; being with you.

- it is how I relent; that makes my dreams seem like they have meaning;

- I finally have a reason for dreams that I have to write down...

Every night...

- my dreams are there to fulfill my need to have you like no one else can....

- - - a mind brimming with a transfixed mirages .... of our departed life;

- - - one that propels my *Ego*; yet makes me weaker by thinking about it

.....one that uplifts my wantonness with my waking vivacity.

Was our bedroom liaisons that *Vital* or;

- were you so sensual, envisioning anything else when I was with you verbose?

- - I have found; both are right!

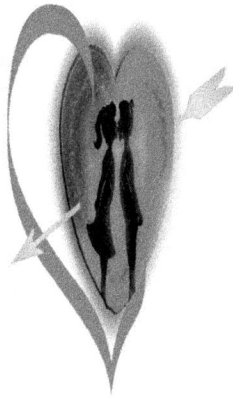

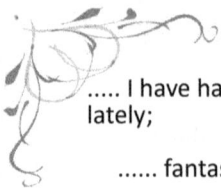

..... I have had the most wonderful dreams of you lately;

...... fantasies that cross the globe;

.... they have been mystical and ethereally risqué

-- these dreams are perpetually how I should please you....

.... *this one was with a twist.*

Dreaming....

We were as usual young and unsure about our needs...

Everything was *Trial* and error;

....Had I known you were thinking about our pleasurable moments as much as I was during my day away, I would have tried to make more of these memorable liaisons.

We were in the city, surrounded by city traffic sights and sounds. The metropolitan skyline made for a great night time back drop to our *Bedroom* lighting. The room is lit with pin lights that accentuate each of the floor to ceiling windows that look out onto the city. It is a beautiful places to get lost in the view just in itself.

Our bed was in the *Center* of this loft style room over looking this city. It felt like we were floating over the city. This makes for an experience that you are in the open for others to see. This lead my dream into a change of importance...

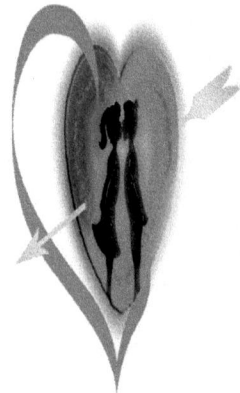

A hushed mood fell over us. Our conversation serene.

We felt like there were others in the room.... not watching just urging us to become more than just lovers. Psychologist might say this was a dream of being a show off. More than showing off, I was in a daze about this whole scene. My mind was telling me what it looked like as another person would have seen us. In front of me was this gorgeous woman that it seemed like I have known for years but our hesitancy at having sex was because we didn't.

Making love felt secondary and there was another reason for my intense curiously into why I was feeling this way. Making love to such a beautiful *Woman* should not have been hard for me. It should have been thought of as an exciting challenge like a sporting event for any guy in my shoes.

This beautiful scene unfolded as we waited to see which one of us will be the first to moan. I of course started so she knew this is exactly what I wanted from her. With her next word, it felt like her hands touched my soul without a clamor. Her hands caressed me like I was literally telling her what to do in my mind and, she reacted without a spoken word.

As we drifted away into shear *Pleasure*... My mind saw you touching me with rays of light that seemed like velvety rose pedals. We were telling each other how this awakened was more pleasurable because, each of us knew instinctively how overwhelming it felt to each of us.

I felt the most pleasure I could have thought possible with your mind speaking to me while we are touching. The room is filled with the glow from the city lights being overtaken by the forthcoming sunrise. Everything is in a glow of rosey orange hue.

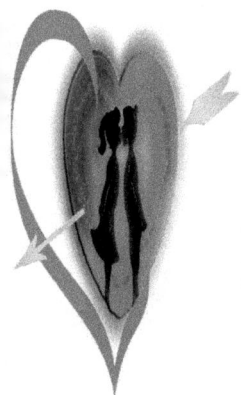

The sky is awakening with glimmers of golden beams of light that seem to overtake my sight of you lying naked next to me.

As the hue brightens, I realize in my dream, I am waking up. My focus is keeping this dream moving forward so I can continue to be apart of this incredible sight of both of us in bed. As causally as the dream started, it began to dissolve. Trying to hang on was useless. It was over.

- - I can no longer be the same person as I once was with you invading my dreams.

...*Intercourse* can never be the same again without having an experience like tonight's dream.

A day at the Beach is different in my dreams....

It is easy to *Tell* a story like this one but, if you have not traveled to the same places that I have..... It needs more *Detail*....

...Since most people haven't traveled to the *Caribbean* and have not seen the endless beauty and nonstop blue water and skies, the nonstop breezes or the sounds of pounding surf ... pummeling the shoreline - no matter where you are ....

the inconceivable ever present set smell of flowers ...I will take for granted that you know all these circumstances are happening all at once in the dream. I can skip these details so you can understand the overall feelings that carried the message of this dream to my waking cognizance.

.... I was married to the most beautiful of *Teen-age* homebody's in my home town. She never was out on her own, never exploded the new or different always stayed at home where it was safe, comfortable reliably mundane.

She became a great *Wife*. Always at home waiting for me to return. It got to the point where my career didn't let me be a home with her as much as she needed me to be, so she sought out another that she could have all to herself.

This brought me to who I am today. Still a workaholic that dreams of having a life that my first wife finally choose for herself.

......My dreams are all I have left of that dissolved romance. My dreams of us are always when we are the same age as when we were married. She turned into a very beautiful woman at only 20 she could have *Won* any beauty contest but; only wanted to keep life real and subdue .... waiting at home for her husband to return home from work ...to be there to great me with a smile and open arms.

Dreaming.....

We are on vacation on one of the *Islands* where I traveled to many times before.

We are getting along like we never left each other's side. My *Number One* is as beautiful as many day in our previous lives together. She is touching my face and holding me while we talking.

The conversation is free and easy without vigilance, like we have never been apart from each other. Caressing turns into *Heavy* petting and I can't resist but to think why aren't we *Making* love right now?

Her face is giving that knowingly *Nod* like she is saying the same thing to herself in my dream. She goes to take my hand and led to a place more our style, the bed where we usually end up after every evening of steady making out.

Instead I grab her and as she turns I toss her gently into the driftwood lounge chairs that are in the center of our palm tree lined, oceanfront hotel terrace. Her body has a glow from the beads of sweat from the sun, as her skin is radiating heat and a glow that seemingly is extremely attractive to me because I am lost in what to do next.

..... My mind (in my dream) is telling me to advance my lusty advance then; that little whisper in the bad of my memories say: slow down I want to drink this all in. I think my mind just want to stay in this moment because at this point there are no consequence of my *Actions*. Moving beyond this point makes both of us to commit to breaking betrothed promises to another.

We lay there in the sun and after a slight of time the natural feeling of being with a first love takes over. As the hurried passion builds the apprehensions of being found out are gone yet; it is only about us two and the time that has passed since we were able to do this.

We are *Entangled* in an embrace, that might be described as one would describe a scene of the passion-entrenched palm leaves waving in the breezes all around us.

Cares faded, loving embraces mingled with fervent sighs and the sun up above is the only thing that we torment.

......Since the dream became a metaphor of how I was feeling about what the consequences of having a relationship with you might be....

......It became my dream but, the *Dream* made me analysis why I was having the dream in the first place.

- I wasn't sorry for coveting you all to myself....

- I repentant that we had the best time - a married couple could have had, even though we were not married to each other....

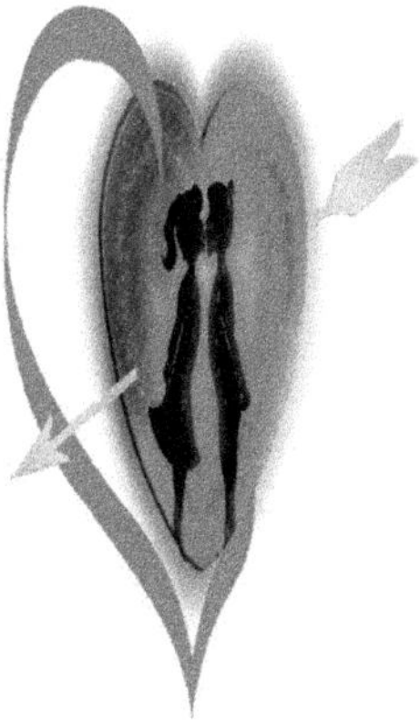

.... It all made for a complicated

Morning!!!

You were my chaperon of dreams....

... What didn't make me blue,

was your night school;

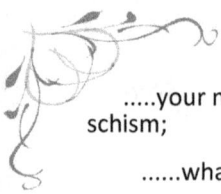

.....your midnight classes, were my evening schism;

......what you *Taught* me, was so cool;

....nothing lit my fire, like listening to your rhythm ....!

...It was over way too fast;

... I needed a long tall one - from your whiskey flask;

..... Southern *Rockin'* .... like an old hound dog;

....to no avail:

.....I hound dogged you .... like he chases his *Tail!*

.....until there was you;

....when my gloom changed into day;

....your love's light shone;

....that spotlight was solely on *Me.*

.... you replenished my wounded heart;

.....even a blind man could tell;

Before you, I was in hell.

.... you taught me how to see;

.....your heartfelt call is now my blinding plea;

for you and I to still be WE!

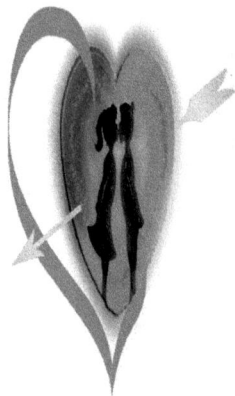

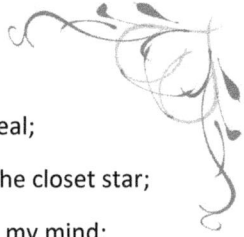

....it makes my *Fantasies* of you real;

.....you are so hot, like a sunspot on the closet star;

....they are forevermore lavished in my mind;

....with your provocative *Zeal*!

if I can;

...I want to indulge in this *Carnal* charm; steamy...

...that I found on our Sunday drive; revelry...

....diving deep, some things are never what they seem; prize...!

....because my *Solitude* was cured with your poise; consciousness...

... you open my eyes to a new way; cognizance..

... I thank God I woke up from this dream; conclusion...

...because I found you beside me; fulfillment

...here comes the my Sun;

.....Ain't no surprise here;

.....it has always been you *Hun*!

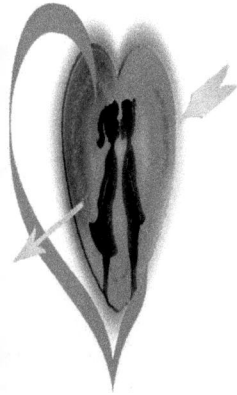

I am without YOU...

standin' in the dark;

....on this bridge between what is *Known* and unknown;

...I thought I'd find you here by now;

..."maybe", "sometime" and "soon" are words that linger.

There is rain;

...it is as long as a *Month* of days;

....my footsteps have been washed away;

...I can't find my way back to YOU;

...memories are gone;

....a *Storm* of tears has washed them from my life.

Everything is a mess;

...MY face is *Willowed*;

....I am still looking for that place;

....where I can find that space;

.... where MY heart was *Blessed*.

Yet again, I am still standing on a bridge alone.

146

I'm searching for a *Myth*;

...one that began with me,

.....grew into we and;

..... is again I alone.

Is there anybody I know here .... *Everything* so confusing;

.....nothing is going steadfast;

....no one wants to be adrift without an anchor;

.....maybe,

....MY mind needs to barren;

....so it can inheriting new *Serenity*.

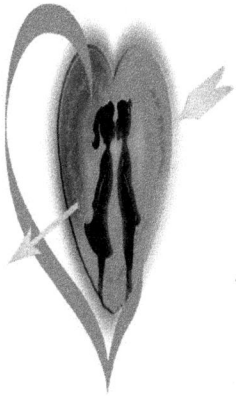

Take the lead, so I can make our way back to WE;

....somewhere new, something to see;

......I don't know who WE are;

....But, *I'm* with YOU!

Chapter

Four:

N.S.F.W.

...for the Fisky ...at Heart!
....If I give my Love to you!

...what the reality of Loving another is like.

Dreams of you have
Tainted my Life:

- - *Life for me will not be the same...*
(N.S.F.W.)

- - these dreams: OMG;

- - - in this one, you and I were in our *Prime*.

.... It starts like many of my days did, you wishing me a good day at work and giving me a little smack on the way to the *Door*.

.... this time you startled me.

It felt normal for me just to walk over to your side of the bed to give you a little kiss good bye, trying to get to the car with my cappuccino in hand and a mind full of traffic that is awaiting.

You were *Playing* a little shy, still tucked up under the covers. What I found was totally the opposite. You were setting me up. You wanted to draw my in *Close*. You knew the more you try to resist me the more I try to get to you. Just like all the times when you play that *"don't Smack my Butt"* and you didn't really mean for me to stop, you just want to egg me *On*. Sometimes the more you resist the more I have to try to tickle you.

So unknowingly, I proceed to get in close ...to get to your tickle spot to make you wake up. To my surprise, you were lying in wait like a lioness *Stalking* tonight's dinner on the plains of Africa.

I close; thinking I was going to grab you and when I got near, the covers slipped down and you had this

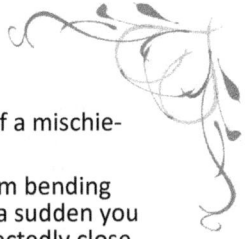

Glimmer in your eyes and the face of a mischievous *Brat*.

As you slip down the sheets and I am bending over to get close enough to you, all of a sudden you grab my head and pull me in so unexpectedly close. You smile like you have plotted this entire morning. You know that what you are about to do is so unexpected, I will treasure the experience forever.

You have my attention and you have my interest and because of this mischievous nod, there is a growing sparkle in my eye. While I am writing encounter down, I am seeing this in my minds eye and can *Never* forget the whole scenario.

You squirm to raise your hand from under the covers. I am becoming intrigued. You glide your fingers across my *Lips* .... slowly and *Intentionally*. This measure of seduction is something that still gets me *Excited*.

The entire time I was getting ready you were thinking about our *Tryst* last night. The memories aroused you to the point you started to massage that spot I love to linger at for hours. Moving them into the wetness ... that must have been so bountiful that it took three fingers to completely accomplish this impulse.

You have been getting your fingers ready for at least five minutes while I am dressing in the bathroom. I *Can't* believe you have done this to me in this morning. This is one of my *Favorite* foreplay things you do to me to make sure I am ready for a protracted love session.

In my dream I am saying to myself....

*...now you are asking for it .... you are going to be sexed up good now - you little *Brat*.*

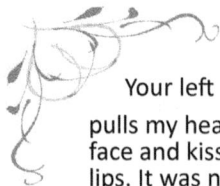

Your left hand comes up out of the covers and pulls my head in closer again. You *Pull* me to your face and kiss me so I can smell your scent on your lips. It was not till then I had a chance to feel you on my lips. The scent of you had me *Stunned* and excited to the point of unconsciousness.

You have taken me by surprise!

You know that this absolutely drives me crazy - to *Know* you have been doing this while I finish dressing. *My sexy little brat is doing this to me and she knows that I won't be leaving for work on time today.*

This leads me to forget all about the awaiting traffic and I begin to kiss you so passionately.

You continue to play the - *Devil* in the *Sheets* - and start to caress my hair bringing your other hand back to my *Lips* to find that you have been dipping these fingers again. Slyly you just brush *Across* my lips and don't let me taste you fingers and float those little tasty digits into your mouth. You grab *My* face and pull me in closer to make sure my eyes can *Share* what you are doing. We love doing this at night before our middling foreplay but, in the *Mornings*, this had never happened.

I am so torn whether just go down on you like a *Crazed* fiend or wait to see what surprises you have in store for me next.

It didn't take long to see you were going to make me VERY late for work today.

I love the flirting and sexual innuendos but, when you *Take* charge and know that this is something

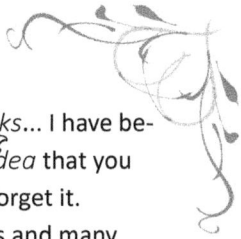

that makes me stop dead in my *Tracks*... I have become so deeply immersed into the *Idea* that you are purposely doing this, I won't ever forget it.

After we trade several damp quests and many deep and unabated *Kisses*, you lift the sheets ever so haltingly so I can see you are wearing the *Skimpiest* and most *Beautifully* tight and shape hugging CFM outfit I have ever seen you *Wear*.

Now, like stunned *Prey* of a lioness, I know you have been planning this morning for some time. I am so turned on because, you have been planning this entire morning planned out and then; *Unleashed* your *Trap* on me.

I can't tell you how immensely and completely in Love with you I am at this moment.

My *Dreams* have been great before, but this time I awoke and started *Writing* this down before I even sent you our morning Bonjour text. I *Can't* believe the *Extravagance* and timing that you taken to prepare and plan for this *Encounter*. I have many, so many dreams of you and I, this one is my favorite because you have planned out this morning in such detailed that it tells me that you enjoy pleasing me in a ways I won't soon forget.

You know what I was doing when I woke up. I had the most pleasurable morning. The *Dream* continued in my twilight wake while I kept the dream playing, over and over again. I can't tell you if I was late for work but, I know I cut the morning coffee time to just one *Cappuccino* before leaving for work. I love the idea that you are there with me in my dreams and every time I have one of you, I always try to tell myself to wake up during the dream

so I don't forget what happened. This one I won't ever forget.

You doing this for me in our past life and now me reliving these situations almost daily, gives me the best reason to smile!

Kiss me like it's our first then, kiss me like it is our last:

It started out to be a beautiful dream of you and me on vacation.

(N.S.F.W.)

...... I'm setting a scene so you can see how beautiful my dream started out.

I was so amazed at the place that I didn't notice what was going on around me.

Imagine you're in *Snow-capped* mountains that are as tall as the Alps but, is not cold outside, it feels wonderful maybe 65-70 degrees.

We are in a Romanesque style building but, probably Byzantine with it's distinctive giant pillars that makes *Cinderella's* castle at Disney look small.

I'm looking at this site from a view up above it all ... like the view from a hawk who has flown down from the sky following the line of the clouds to the

pillars .... along the castle's pillar tops and down to a courtyard.... It is a White-stone courtyard that's where Y*ou* and I now are.

The courtyard is surrounded by candles... it's strange how there are like candles but they are floating all around us. The Courtyard has a stone railing the separates the looming drop off the side of the castle and the *Courtyard*.

The Sun is already setting and it's basically dusk. The candles get brighter not just brighter but more beautiful so I can see you in a glow that is haunting but, makes for a very beautiful scene.

Their glow doesn't make your skin pale it just gives your entire face, arms and legs....oh, those legs... a bright beautiful rosy shimmer.

You have on a dress made from feathery light *Chiffon* material, the kind of *Flows* with any kind of wind but, the white color of the dress is now a pinkish-pale hue because the lighting from the candle's flames. The courtyard is *Shimmering* all - around with flickering lights bouncing off the white-stone walls.

Your dress is flowing all the way down to your ankles where I can just see you have on some really nice stiletto *Heels* ... which I know, when I take a look at your butt later, will make that dress extremely tight in the rear, so I can see every curve.

I think to myself I love it when you wear *High heels* I just don't know how I'm going to sneak around to see that butt of yours without making it completely obvious that I'm just staring at your *Butt*..

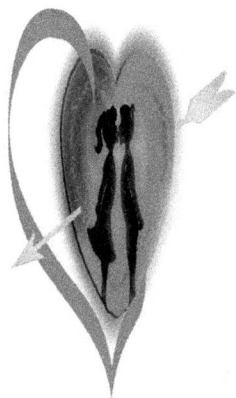

Somehow I stop about thinking about that butt because I see your tighten your grip around me ... you are *Hugging* me and I didn't even know how it happened so quick.

As I'm dreaming this I'm seeing both of us in this clutch .... viewing this from a another person's point of view from above .... *I* can see it as if we were steps away. I see that you are making it plainly obvious that you want to grab a hold of me and initiate the first kiss.

You say something to me but I can't understand the words, I'm just so wrapped up and thinking about what is going on right here in front of me, you are so *Beautiful*, I can't concentrate on what you're saying to me.

I can't believe you're a you're talking to me and I can't hear what you're saying and then in my dream I flow back out again to see this scene from afar and I know why I can't hear you .. I'm so *Beguiled* by your butt ... I think my mind is just wondering... and I can't concentrate to listen.

Then, I feel it, your arms are so in tangled around my head because have grabbed my head with your hands and arms and pulled them to you so you can kiss me so hard ..... your arms are now blocking my ears .... I can't hear sounds because they are being muffled by your arms that have closed off my ears because- you have wrapped them so hard around my head.

This entire time I see this going on in a second person point of view. I'm watching what's going on and then I realize this and I tell myself in my *Dream* to move your head so I can hear what

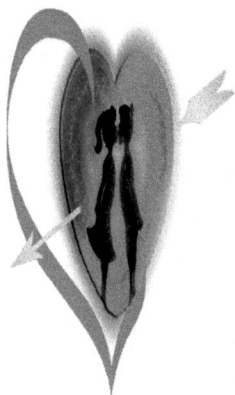

you're saying. I move my head so your arms are not blocking my ears and I hear the last couple things you say to me

"Kiss me like the first time that we ever kissed and, then I want you to Kiss me like it is our last time that we Ever do this again."

I lost track of time and my hands just cannot slow down because they're working so hard to tear away your clothes but in a way that never seems to end .... These layers of chiffon just keep replenishing themselves and doesn't seem like I ever get to feel your *Bare* body.

I finally learned that I need to spin you around and I as I'm doing this, then I turn you and exposure back to me then, I can see how beautiful your nearly bare figure is in a candle light. In those high heels your rear just look so delectable I'm thinking to my-self I cannot wait any longer.

Starting at the top your neck and work on their way down your shoulders to your arms my left hand finds the center of your back and it just push you forward slightly against the rough stone railing that is separating the courtyard and the castle walls and the huge expanse of extremely gorgeous of Moun-tain-crested views, looming just past the rail is a perilous drop to the mountain prairie below. This is always been just in front of us. It is a beautiful sight with the snow-capped mountains in the background.

I am lost at the *View* of your body in front of me ....this beautiful sensual woman with a flowing

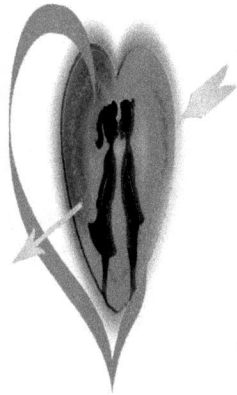

chiffon dress that floats seductively across your limbs with any whisper of a breeze…. That material just barely floating around you, lingering over your body as I am gently pushing you forward nearer to a abbess.

As I'm getting my hands down your back I find your waist and then both of my hands *Caress* your butt, it is so beautiful and the site of it in the candlelight …. with your skin simmering, I can just see that not only is this a beautiful sight for my eyes but you know it's giving me a passion-jolt looking at your *Bunda*.

I can't help myself I start kissing your back from your neck around the collarbone to the back of your neck.

Quickly I'm traveling down the middle of your back to where I have to drop to my *Knees* and I'm pushing your Bunda more towards me … it's wonderful.

You are so beautiful and I just can't believe that my wife and I are in this castle courtyard and about to have *Sex* - where anybody could be looking at us….

It's just one of those things… I know we're safe and no one's going to disturb us but, it's just that moment that I want to dive … in between your legs with my kisses and this is where somehow my dream changes and we find ourselves in a bed and you know what happens … I start and I just don't stop licking and sucking on your *Sex*.

…you cannot have me going down on you anymore without feeling Me inside you.

Now that we somehow move from the courtyard into a bedroom you feel so much more comfortable, you relax and the sex just gets better and better I don't want to tell you how long it seems

like *20*.... *30* maybe *45* minutes we just never seem to stop. I'm there and your sex is just so great feeling I cannot tell you how wonderful soft you are... like velvet glove that doesn't want to give up holding me inside you.

I'm amazed at how long I've been doing this without having to finish ... I just wanted to last ... forever.

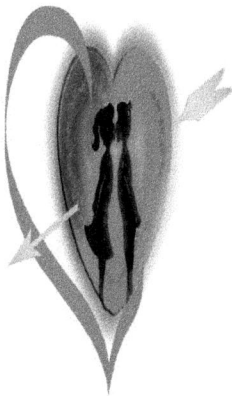

I have you surrounded by my arms there holding on to you and then **you** say I cannot stop this without showing you what *I* want to do with you.... things that you never were able to do before with me when we were younger and unsure. I am grinning from ear to ear because I'm so happy that you can say this to me

My thoughts are... what is she saying to me?? ...what do you want to do to me and inside my mind ... while I am still dreaming....

I'm just thinking about all these things that we could be doing and you push yourself away from me and you move around and you completely turn around and I'm lying flat on my back now you're on top of me riding me in a backwards position so I can see your butt move up and down on *Me*.

Of course you know this is too much for me to handle and you only do it for a few times because watching your butt wiggle up and down in front of

me like that this going to be too much for me to handle in I'm going to burst .... you know that I don't want to do that now because in my dream we have this unspoken communication ... you just know by the way I feel and you know that I'm going to orgasm but you say stop and you say *we're not ready yet*.

Your ass is still in front of me and have to *Grab* it. I bring it towards me and I start sucking on your *Thang* and I am so relentless and of course you start on me and you are so talented with your mouth ... doing me even better and more skilled than I remember from when we were younger. I'm about ready and I tell you that I'm going to orgasm in your mouth. You grab my ass with both your hands pull me closer and force me further into your mouth.

Your ass is *Wiggling* on my face and it is like you know that I can't hold off any longer but you stop sucking on me and start biting instead. *Nibbling* it first and then you grab a hold of me with your fist. I am about ready to explode and you clinch down with your fist you say no! You can't finish until I say you can.

I'm so hard in your hand and it looks so tiny gripping me the way it is but you have such a tight grip it *Hurts* but it hurts so good ... if you know what I mean... ;-)

I am thrilled that you are not afraid to take charge. I'm *Happy* that we have made it to this point where we're both comfortable with what we are doing to each other. We are both feeling great right now .... we are comfortable being in the controller and a *Controlled*.

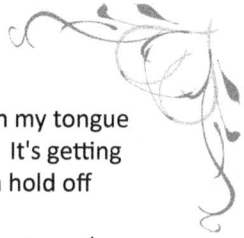

I want to control your orgasms with my tongue and lips and you want to control mine. It's getting to the point where I don't know if I can hold off anymore.

This is such a situation it is got me so turned on with you being in *Command* of this situation and leading the charge ... when it used to be **me** and now we're **equal** partners in *Pleasing* each other, it is *Amazing*.

I'm there ready to bust and ready to absolutely start this all over again ... and you stop tickling me with your teeth and start teasing me and never thought it was possible for you to get better but, you are! I don't know how but, *You* are!

I want to stop and explode at the same time, I want to do both and do it over and over again. My dream starts going into a repeating mode.

Every 3 minutes this scene replayed and then repeating another 2 or 3 minutes. It is like I'm on auto reverse on a VHS tape. I just replay it over and over again because it is so, so ... nice. It is a situation where you feel so comfortable and I am so glad that we are able to be so comfortable together... it just seems like my mind is saying I never *Want* this to end and I just keep replaying it 3rd or 4th time in my head...

I end up having you get off of me and then I am bending you over the bed and we are doing it over the edge of the bed and I have your one leg up so I can fit into your tightness. It feels so warm so hot and it feels like your hand again is wrapped around me and it's actually your vagina that is tight and pulsating.

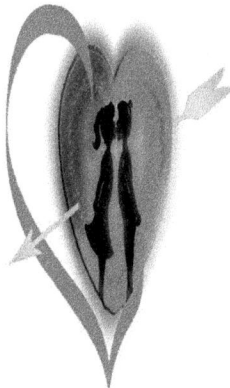

I am dreaming and realize I'm in a dream I am pulsating not you. Then you drop your leg down and you pull both your legs together tight and we're still in the throes of rapid sessions of punching deeper and deeper. I feel like there's an ocean of hands wrapped around my member and I can't describe what it's like to be inside you but I can tell you it is not like other women that I've had.

Your legs are closed tight and is making me wonder how I can possibly last this long and then it comes down to the point where I cannot hold off any *Longer* and I tell you that I have to have this moment with you and you say I know....! I've been waiting for you to ask me so we can have this moment together.

I want to reach around to grab your face and bring it towards mind and kiss you so passionately but you're facing the other direction I have no other way to do this but to stop with the rocking motion. I grab your face and pull it closer. This scenario is more fantastic than any other sex episode in my life and I tell you this in my dream.

My hands are gathering you towards me and *Forcing* us onto your vagina. No way that this is any possibility of this situation ever happening to me again in real life because, it is so wonderful, it is so beautiful for me to see you in bed with me. It is a *Wonderful* feeling of having you in my arms and holding you so tight being so intimate.... we are slowly finishing and I am so spent and you have such a content look.

After I have you facing me I can see your lips, I just need to touch them again. Your *Eyes* I'm staring into them .... I feel like I lost five minutes just

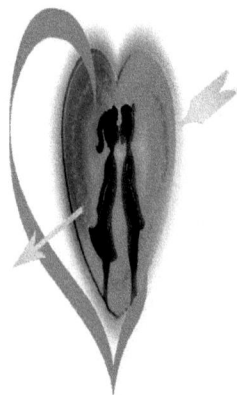

gazing into them. This is something that never happened to me before.

I can't even begin to tell you how this is changing the way I think about having sex again.

It's no longer sex ...it is being with my wife and this love making is no longer just having sex, it is now living a life of love with a wife, a wife that I always knew was right there in my grasp but I couldn't get the right words out ......to hold on to you.

It feels like I lost an important part of *Me* ... being able to express love through and, with my wife. What is slipping away from me is my love life, my wife, the one that I held so dearly at one time and now it seems like it's all a dream.

Now I'm kissing that girl in my dreams like I will never see her again....

My favorite dreams are of you:

_I woke today before the Sun with this
beautiful thought of you._
_(N.S.F.W.)_
_I know this because I took notes as soon as I
finished this dream._

It started out like most dreams of you, we are so
relaxed having a great sex adventure..... We are as
usual - young ...
This is how it came to me:

It is quite and not *Set* in any of our previous
places from any my dreams of you. We are in the
home on Limerick drive. I am playing with you in
bed.

...you are so beautiful, just poised with your knees
on both sides of my head, ready to smash your sex
down on my face.

You first have been telling me what you are going
to do to me ahead of doing it..... I am loving your
bold confidence and sexual desire for me to pleasure
you.

You are about to settled down, then you start to
tease me some more because you know what I want
to do to you!!!

.....I am so waiting for this..... *Because*, you
have been readying me for the last few minutes with
your talking dirty to me.... before, actually getting in
to it.

In this dream, just like so many other nights
when we were together, you have on the skimpiest,
sexiest, lacy undies .....you always had such a beauti-

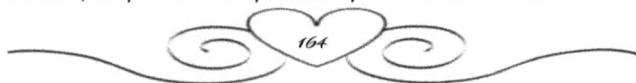

ful array of bedroom nighties...then, again your ass in a tee shirt did enough for me most of the times.

..... *always love the high 𝓗eels too.*

...you wore these 𝒰ndies....they were so beautiful, almost see through, I can just see you gorgeous *thang* underneath the material.

You reach around to make sure I am hard from this and of course you say, "this is what I am going to *lollipop*" - after you are done getting head from me.

You bring your other hand down and start to massage your undies and they are just a little damp because after all the times we have done this in the past, you know how much I love giving you 𝓗ead.

.... your sex is awaiting my tongue; you push a finger or two into the material so I can see that it is getting wetter.

I am getting so tempted to just grab you and force you down on my tongue but hesitate because we play like this a lot. I see you lift the material away and I can finally see your creaming 𝒯hang. I am so turned on because you are still playing with it using your fingers ferociously. .....all-the-while, I can see your fingers are getting wetter.

I know what I want but you tempt me first with a taste of your fingers. I am 𝒟evouring your orgasm from your fingers. It is such a turn on because it brings me back to that time ...I did this all night long last week.

....We both know it is why you are doing this. You know it will remind me of our previous encounters where I have - 𝒴ou - touch yourself so I can devour your wet fingers. I am at the point that I want you to smash your sex on my face soon.

You gently push aside the material away from your sex and move down closer to my mouth. I am reaching a breaking point, you grab my head with both hands and say to me ...

"I don't want just your ✑*ongue,*
I need all of you in me"

....You grab the back of my head with both hands and pull me to you as you lower towards my ✑*outh.* You start by rocking slowly, then start a more profuse grinding motion. It is like you want my face to totally be engulfed.

I absolutely love YOUR intensity. You are so soft and so ✑*elvety* tender. It is like I am tasting you for the first time.... It has been forever since I have had such an experience and it still reminds me of the best sex we'd ever had.

Your sex so cozy .... but, I force my tongue deep. I want to give you a climax ... *so strong that your grandmothers gynecologist feels it* .... I want to feel you orgasming from the top of my tongue to the middle of my throat.

I want to feel legs buckle and contract

around my head...

✑*hen;*

...you shutter a little and I know this isn't as much as you need right now. What I was going for I want to trip your trigger, one that makes you want to write me a thank you letter, penned in your own wetness so, I can smell your excitement when I open it.

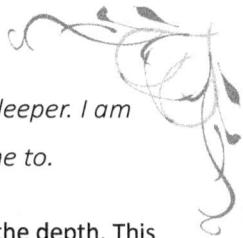

You pull my hair and force me in deeper. I am

responding like you need me to.

My *Quickness* is matched only by the depth. This is when I begin to wake up. I am thinking about this over and over in my head.

.....Laying there I hear a passing jet and the rain *Dripping* from the roof.

....I know I am not asleep yet awake enough to feel my hardness growing. So I begin to replay this scene over and, over and, over ....my hardness can't be controlled.... I know I have to masturbate right then because I NEED TO finish the rest of the dream while stroking off to this scene *Replaying* in my head.

While I work to a climax the dream develops. I am fantasizing about how it should continue...... I know you are getting ready to come all over my face...... I want it to play out in my head while I am in this twilight sleep.

I feel myself getting harder as I think about getting you to orgasm for me. I can start to *Feel* your legs tighten around my head and now I feel IT IS YOUR hands that are working me to a climax.

My legs tighten. I can hear my breath quicken, getting deeper and getting louder. I am wondering if the TV in the other room is loud enough so no one can hear me.

I am under your *Control*. This morning like so many other times, you are making my face wet. You are squeezing my head and gripping handfuls of hair....

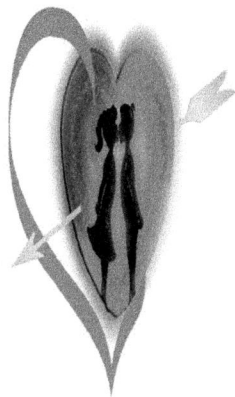

....this is the time when both of us should orgasm. .....as if you were the with me, I begin to feel my heart quicken and know it is just a few more strokes. I am using only a few fingers because it reminds of your tiny hands.

In this Twilight I can feel you
climax on my tongue.

You are rocking your thang across my Mouth and I can hear muffled squealing, even though your thighs that are squeezing my head and is blocking my ears.

.....I can't hear much because - your legs are so tightly wrapped around my ears but, I can tell you are enjoying my head - that I am giving you.

The din of these muted sounds get me ready to orgasm with you. I tell you I am orgasming too and you pull away just in time to catch the first few of my pearls. My breathing has almost halted because this orgasm is so strong I can't even concentrate on anything but you crushing your sex down onto my mouth. What a beautiful feeling.

You aren't pushing me away. You want me to drive your orgasm to another level.

You reach around to grab me and

Tell me it is my turn now.

I Love You.

Fred Garvin....

.....Your Manslut for Evermore.

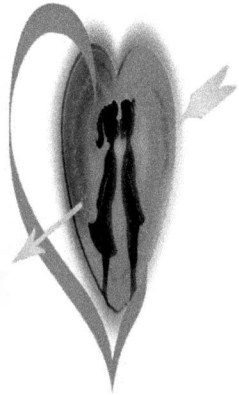

The
End